Illustrator:
Ken Tunell

Editors:
Barbara M. Wally, M.S.
Dona Herweck Rice

Editorial Project Manager:
Ina Massler Levin, M.A.

Editor in Chief:
Sharon Coan, M.S. Ed.

Art Director:
Elayne Roberts

Associate Designer:
Denise Bauer

Art Coordination Assistant:
Cheri Macoubrie Wilson

Cover Artist:
Larry Bauer

Product Manager:
Phil Garcia

Imaging:
Ralph Olmedo, Jr.

Researcher:
Christine Johnson

Publishers:
Rachelle Cracchiolo, M.S. Ed.
Mary Dupuy Smith, M.S. Ed.

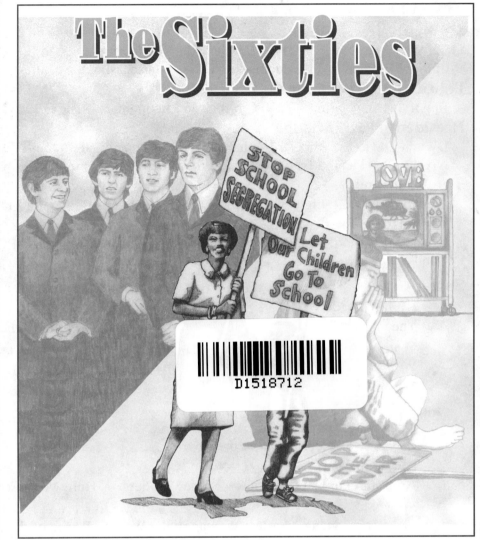

Author:

Mary Ellen Sterling, M.Ed.

Teacher Created Materials, Inc.
6421 Industry Way
Westminster, CA 92683
www.teachercreated.com
©*1998 Teacher Created Materials, Inc.*
Reprinted, 2000
Made in U.S.A.
ISBN-1-57690-028-2

Table of Contents

Table of Contents *(cont.)*

Introduction

The 20th Century is a series which examines the political, economic, social, cultural, scientific, and technological advances of the twentieth century and introduces students to the individuals who made history in each decade.

The Sixties chronicles a decade of rapid change and rebellion in America. As the decade began, Americans responded with hope and enthusiasm to the challenge made by charismatic president John Kennedy. Many joined the Peace Corps, a volunteer agency established to help developing nations worldwide. Others devoted themselves to the cause of civil rights in America. When Kennedy was assasinated in 1963, the entire country was shocked and saddened. Vice President Lyndon Johnson became president. Although he guided the passage of strong civil rights and economic opportunity acts, Johnson could not command the hearts of Americans as Kennedy had.

Following the Gulf of Tonkin incident in 1964, American involvement in South Vietnam's struggle against communist-held North Vietnam escalated. Many Americans, especially young people, protested against this war and against the draft. The war and the controversy surrounding it lasted into the seventies.

Discouraged by the slow pace of change through nonviolence, blacks turned to new leaders who advocated Black Power. Frustration led to violent confrontations and riots in major cities. Martin Luther King, Jr. was assasinated in 1968.

Cesar Chavez organized the United Farm Workers to protest the unsafe conditions and low wages of migrant workers, while Betty Friedan led the women's liberation movement.

This unit includes the following:

- ❑ a time line—a chronology of significant events of the decade
- ❑ planning guides—summaries and suggested activities for introducing the key issues and events of the decade
- ❑ personality profiles—brief biographies of important individuals of the decade
- ❑ chronology of world events of the decade
- ❑ language experience ideas—suggestions for writing and vocabulary building
- ❑ group activities—assignments to foster cooperative learning
- ❑ topics for further research—suggestions for extending the unit
- ❑ literature connections—summaries of related books and suggested activities for expanding them
- ❑ curriculum connections—activities in math, art, language arts, social studies, and music
- ❑ computer applications— suggestions for selecting and using software to supplement this unit
- ❑ bibliography—suggestions for additional resources on the decade

> To keep this valuable resource intact so that it can be used year after year, you may wish to punch holes in the pages and store them in a three-ring binder.

Time Line

	1960	1961
Politics and Economics	• President: Dwight D. Eisenhower Vice president: Richard M. Nixon • The 50-star flag becomes official on July 4, 1960. John F. Kennedy wins the 1960 presidential election. Hearings on the "payola" scandal are held in Congress. A U-2 spy plane piloted by Gary Powers is shot down by the Russians.	• John F. Kennedy is inaugurated as the 36th president of the United States; Lyndon B. Johnson is his vice president. • Diplomatic relations with Cuba are severed. • The Bay of Pigs invasion fails. • The Peace Corps is established.
Social and Cultural	The United States Post Office Department establishes the first automated post office. Chrysler discontinues its DeSoto line of cars. Four debates between presidential candidates Kennedy and Nixon are televised. Cesar Chavez forms the United Farm Workers. The first sit-in to protest racial segregation is held.	Freedom Riders are attacked by white mobs. The Berlin Wall is built in Germany.
Science and Technology	The first geothermal power plant produces electricity. The first contraceptive pills are marketed in the United States. The first nuclear powered aircraft carrier, the *Enterprise*, is launched.	IBM markets the Selectric® typewriter with changeable type. Two American helicopter companies are sent to Vietnam. The first American astronaut, Alan Shepard, makes a suborbital space flight.

Time Line *(cont.)*

1962	1963	1964
Riots erupt as African American James Meredith enrolls at the University of Mississippi.	Medgar Evers, an official with the NAACP, is shot by a sniper.	President Johnson declares "War on Poverty."
The Twenty-fourth Amendment is approved.	The Supreme Court rules that prayer in public schools is unconstitutional.	The Civil Rights Act is passed.
The Nuclear Test Ban Treaty goes into effect on October 10.	President Kennedy is assassinated; Lyndon Johnson is sworn in as President.	The Warren Report concludes that Lee Harvey Oswald acted alone in assassinating President Kennedy.
October 16–28 the Cuban Missile Crisis takes place.		The Twenty-fourth Amendment is ratified, making poll taxes illegal in federal elections.
		Nikita Khrushchev is deposed as leader of the Soviet Union.
		Congress passes the Gulf of Tonkin Resolution.
Jackie Kennedy takes the public on a tour of the White House via television.	African Americans demonstrate in the March on Washington.	Martin Luther King, Jr., is awarded the Nobel Peace Prize.
Chubby Checker starts a new national dance craze—the Twist.	Martin Luther King, Jr., delivers his "I have a dream . . ." speech.	The Beatles make their first United States appearance on CBS television on the *Ed Sullivan Show*.
Powdered orange juice is introduced.	*The Feminine Mystique* is published.	Simon and Garfunkel release their first album, *Wednesday Morning, 3 A.M.*
A Braille typewriter for use by the blind is developed.	Jack Ruby kills accused presidential assassin Lee Harvey Oswald.	In a major upset Cassius Clay knocks out Sonny Liston.
	The Post Office introduces the ZIP code.	Teamster leader Jimmy Hoffa negotiates the first national contract between Teamsters and trucking companies.
John Glenn becomes the first American to orbit the earth.	A vaccine against measles (*rubeola*) is developed.	The Verrazano-Narrows Bridge opens in New York City. It is the largest suspension bridge of its day.
NASA launches *Telstar*, a communication satellite, for AT&T.	Kodak markets the Instamatic camera, which uses a film cartridge.	
	Polaroid introduces a Polacolor camera.	

Time Line *(cont.)*

1965	1966	1967
Lyndon Johnson is inaugurated for his second term in office; Hubert Humphrey is his vice president.	E. W. Brooke of Massachusetts becomes the first African American in the United States Senate in 85 years.	The Twenty-fifth Amendment is passed on February 10, 1967.
Riots in Watts cause 35 deaths and millions of dollars in damages.	U. S. participation in Vietnam escalates.	The first endangered species list is published by the Department of Interior.
Martin Luther King, Jr., leads a Selma to Montgomery march on March 21–25.	The former British colony of Barbados becomes independent.	
Johnson's "Great Society" opens with the passing of Medicare and the Water Quality Act.	Ronald Reagan, future United States president, is elected governor of California.	
	Robert Weaver becomes the first Secretary of Housing and Urban Development. He is the first black member of the cabinet.	
African American leader Malcolm X is shot and killed.	The National Safety Board is established to set standards for automobiles.	Three United States astronauts are killed in a flash fire at Cape Kennedy, Florida.
Cesar Chavez leads migrant workers in a strike against grape growers.	LSD is introduced into the drug culture.	The number of United States troops in Vietnam now stands at 474,300. Demonstrations for and against the Vietnam War are held in New York City.
Lawyer and consumer advocate Ralph Nader publishes *Unsafe at Any Speed*, a critical look at American automobiles.	The Motion Picture Academy introduces a code for films.	The United States population reaches 200 million.
The Beatles begin their first United States tour on February 7.	Huey Newton and other black activists found the Black Panther Party.	African Americans riot in Detroit, Newark, and other cities.
The Grateful Dead, featuring Jerry Garcia, is founded.	NOW (National Organization for Women) is founded.	The summer of "flower power" is celebrated.
	The Supreme Court decision of *Miranda V. Arizona* affirms the rights of defendants in criminal cases.	The first Super Bowl game is played.
		British model Twiggy appears in New York City.
The videocassette recorder is developed.	Dr. De Bakey installs the first artificial heart pump.	Insulin is the first human protein to be synthesized.
Super-8 mm movie cameras and film cassettes are developed.	The American *Gemini 8* spacecraft achieves the first docking in space.	Overseas direct dialing begins.
Ray Dolby develops a method of reducing background noise in recordings.		Computer keyboards are developed, replacing punched cards, punched tapes, and magnetic tapes.
The first American walks in space.		

Time Line

	Politics and Economics	Social and Cultural	Science and Technology
1969	Richard M. Nixon is inaugurated as the 37th president; Spiro T. Agnew is his vice president. Nixon announces plans to withdraw troops from Vietnam. By September, 55,000 American soldiers leave Vietnam.	Charles Manson's cult murders Sharon Tate and others. The Trial of the Chicago Seven gets underway. Buildings at Harvard University are seized by 400 striking students. The Woodstock Music and Art Fair is held in New York. Hell's Angels attack hippies during a Rolling Stones concert at Altamont Speedway. In a dispute over censorship, *The Smothers Brothers* television show is cancelled. *Sesame Street*, featuring the Muppets, begins on Public Television.	A vaccine against rubella is approved by the FDA. American astronauts Neil Armstrong and Buzz Aldrin are the first to walk on the moon.
1968	The *USS Pueblo* is seized by North Korea. Martin Luther King, Jr., is assassinated. President Johnson announces he will not seek re-election. North Vietnam launches a massive Tet offensive. Robert F. Kennedy, presidential candidate, is assassinated on June 5. Republican Richard Nixon narrowly defeats Democratic candidate Hubert Humphrey.	Fights erupt at the Democratic National Convention in Chicago between police and anti-war protestors. Leaders of the Yippies are arrested. U.S. postage is raised to six cents for standard first class letters. Student riots are widespread. Yale admits women students for the first time. *60 Minutes*, a news magazine, debuts on television.	*Apollo 8* completes the first United States manned mission to the moon. The first live television broadcast from space is aired.

Using the Time Line

Use pages five to eight to create a visual display for your classroom. Follow the steps outlined below to assemble the time line as a bulletin board display and then choose from the suggested uses those that best suit your classroom needs.

Bulletin Board Assembly

Copy pages five to eight. Enlarge and/or color them, if desired. Tape the pages together to form a continuous time line and attach it to a prepared bulletin board background or a classroom wall. (To make a reusable bulletin board, glue each page of the time line to oaktag. After the glue has dried, laminate the pages. Write on the laminated pages with dry erase markers.)

	1960	1961	1962	1963	1964	1965	1966	1967	1968	1969	
Politics and Economics	President: Dwight D. Eisenhower. Vice president: Richard M. Nixon. The 50-star flag becomes official on July 4, 1960. John F. Kennedy wins the 1960 presidential election. Hearings on the "payola" scandal are held in Congress. A U-2 spy plane piloted by Gary Powers is shot down by the Russians.	John F. Kennedy is inaugurated as the 35th president of the United States. Lyndon B. Johnson is his vice president. Diplomatic relations with Cuba are severed. The Bay of Pigs invasion fails. The Peace Corps is established.	Riots erupt as African American James Meredith enrolls at the University of Mississippi. The Supreme Court rules that prayer in public schools is unconstitutional. The Nuclear Test Ban Treaty goes into effect on October 10. October 16–28 the Cuban Missile Crisis takes place.	Medgar Evers, an official with the NAACP, is shot by a sniper. The Supreme Court rules that poor defendants are entitled to assistance of counsel. President Kennedy is assassinated; Lyndon Johnson is sworn in as President.	President Johnson declares "War on Poverty." The Civil Rights Act is passed. The Warren Report concludes that Lee Harvey Oswald acted alone in assassinating President Kennedy. The Twenty-Fourth Amendment is ratified, making poll taxes illegal in federal elections. Nikita Khrushchev is deposed as leader of the Soviet Union. Congress passes the Gulf of Tonkin Resolution.	Lyndon Johnson is inaugurated for his second term in office; Hubert Humphrey is his vice president. U.S. participation in Vietnam escalates. Riots in Watts cause 35 deaths and millions of dollars in damages. Martin Luther King, Jr., leads a Selma to Montgomery march on March 21–25. Johnson's "Great Society" opens with the passing of Medicare and the Water Quality Act.	E. W. Brooke of Massachusetts becomes the first African American in the United States Senate in 85 years. The former British colony of Barbados becomes independent. Ronald Reagan, future United States president, is elected governor of California. Robert Weaver becomes the first Secretary of Housing and Urban Development. He is the first black member of the cabinet.	The Twenty-fifth Amendment is passed on February 10, 1967. The first endangered species list is published by the Department of Interior.	The USS Pueblo is seized by North Korea. Martin Luther King, Jr., is assassinated. President Johnson announces he will not seek re-election. North Vietnam launches a massive Tet offensive. Robert F. Kennedy, presidential candidate, is assassinated on June 5. Nixon announces plans to withdraw troops from Vietnam. By September, 30,000 American soldiers leave Vietnam.	Richard M. Nixon is inaugurated as the 37th president; Spiro T. Agnew is his vice president. Republican Richard Nixon narrowly defeats Democratic candidate Hubert Humphrey.	**Politics and Economics**
Social and Cultural	The first geothermal power plant produces electricity. The United States Post Office Department publishes the first automated post office. Chrysler discontinues its DeSoto line of cars. Four debates between presidential candidates Kennedy and Nixon are televised. Cesar Chavez forms the United Farm Workers. The first sit-in to protest racial segregation is held.	Freedom Riders are attacked by white mobs. The Berlin Wall is built in Germany.	Jackie Kennedy takes the public on a tour of the White House via television. Chubby Checker starts a new national dance craze—the Twist. The Aventine Mystique is published. Jack Ruby kills accused presidential assassin Lee Harvey Oswald. The Post Office introduces the ZIP code.	African Americans demonstrate in the March on Washington. Martin Luther King, Jr., delivers his "I have a dream..." speech. Simon and Garfunkel release their first album, Wednesday Morning, 3 A.M. A Braille typewriter for use by the blind is developed.	Martin Luther King, Jr., is awarded the Nobel Peace Prize. The Beatles make their first United States appearance on CBS television on the Ed Sullivan Show.	Cesar Chavez leads migrant workers in a strike against grape growers. Lawyer and consumer advocate Ralph Nader publishes Unsafe at Any Speed, a critical look at American automobiles. The Beatles begin their first United States tour on February 7. The Grateful Dead, featuring Jerry Garcia, is founded.	The National Safety Board is established to set standards for automobiles. The Motion Picture Academy introduces a code for films. Huey Newton and other black activists found the Black Panther Party. NOW (National Organization for Women) is founded. The Supreme Court affirms the rights of defendants in criminal cases.	Three United States astronauts are killed in a flash fire at Cape Kennedy, Florida. The number of United States troops in Vietnam now stands at 474,300. Demonstrations for and against the Vietnam War continue. The United States population reaches 200 million. African Americans riot in Detroit, Newark, and other cities. The summer of "flower power" is celebrated.	Fights erupt at the Democratic National Convention in Chicago between police and anti-war protestors. Leaders of the Yippies are arrested. The Woodstock Music and Art Fair is held in New York. U.S. postage is raised to six cents for standard first class letters. Student riots are widespread. Yale admits women students for the first time.	Charles Manson's cult murders Sharon Tate and others. The Trial of the Chicago Seven gets underway. Buildings at Harvard University are seized by 400 striking students. The Woodstock Music and Art Fair is held in New York. Hell's Angels attack hippies during a Rolling Stones concert at Altamont Speedway. In a dispute over censorship, The Smothers Brothers television show is cancelled. Sesame Street, featuring the Muppets, begins on Public Television.	**Social and Cultural**
Science and Technology	The first geothermal power plant produces electricity. The first contraceptive pills are marketed in the United States. The first nuclear powered aircraft carrier, the Enterprise, is launched.	IBM markets the Selectric typewriter with changeable type. Two American helicopter companies are sent to Vietnam. The first American astronaut, Alan Shepard, makes a suborbital space flight.	John Glenn becomes the first American to orbit the earth. NASA launches Telstar, a communication satellite, for AT&T.	Instant color photography (Polaroid) is introduced. Polaroid introduces a Polacolor camera.	The Verrazano-Narrows Bridge opens in New York City. It is the largest suspension bridge of its day.	The videophone recorder is developed. Super-8 mm movie cameras and film cassettes are developed. Ray Dolby develops a method of reducing background noise in recordings. The first American walks in space.	Insulin is the first human protein to be synthesized. Overseas direct dialing begins. Computer keyboards are developed, replacing punched cards, punched tapes, and magnetic tapes.	Dr. De Bakey installs the first artificial heart pump. The first live television broadcast from space is aired.	Apollo 8 completes the first United States manned mission to the moon.	A vaccine against rubella is approved by the FDA. American astronauts Neil Armstrong and Buzz Aldrin are the first to walk on the moon.	**Science and Technology**

Suggested Uses

1. Use the time line to assess students' initial knowledge of the era. Construct a web to find out what they know about Vietnam or women's liberation, for example. Find out what they would like to know. Plan your lessons accordingly.

2. Assign each group of students a specific year. As they research that year, let them add pictures, names, and events to the appropriate area of the time line.

3. Assign the students to find out what events were happening around the world during the 1960s. Tell them to add that information to the bottom of the time line.

4. After adding new names, places, and events to the time line, use the information gathered as a study guide for assessment. Base your quizzes and exams on those people, places, and events which you have studied.

5. After the time line has been on display for a few days, begin to quiz students about the people, places, and events named on the time line. Call on one student at a time to stand so that he or she is facing away from the actual time line. Ask a question based on the information. **Variation:** Let the students compose the questions.

6. Use the time line as a springboard for class discussions—for example, who was the most famous or influential person of the 1960s? How has the Vietnam War impacted their lives? What effect did women's liberation have on future generations? How was life in the 1960s similar to life today?

7. Divide the students into three groups and assign each group a different area: politics/economics, social/cultural, and science/technology. Have each group brainstorm important related people, places, and events that occurred during the sixties, and then create a group mural depicting these important happenings. Get permission to decorate a hallway wall or tape several sheets of butcher paper together to make a giant canvas.

8. Assign groups of students to make specialized time lines, for example, a time line of space exploration, a time line of events in the civil rights movement, or a time line of Vietnam War events.

Sixties Overview

- In his inaugural address John F. Kennedy challenged Americans, especially young adults, to work for change. Many devoted themselves to the cause of social justice by joining the Peace Corps, while others helped register black voters in Mississippi.

- Legislation in the 1950s had provided for school integration. In the 1960s, attention was focused on eliminating discrimination in all public places and in employment and on guaranteeing the right to vote. Powerful black leaders emerged and gathered their people to demonstrate against the injustices they had been enduring. They waged their campaign with sit-ins, marches, and other nonviolent means but were often subjected to beatings, bombings, and even shootings.

- The new serious attitudes of young people called for a different style of music. Folk singers with acoustic guitars sang traditional ballads. A new group of young folk artists created new songs about current social problems. These "protest" singers, including Bob Dylan, Joan Baez, and Phil Ochs, often appeared at civil rights and antiwar demonstrations.

- Kennedy's assassination in 1963 shocked and saddened the country.

- The new president, Lyndon Johnson, declared an "unconditional war on poverty" in his first state of the union address and guided the passage of a strong Civil Rights Act and an Economic Opportunity Act.

- Attention focused on the Southeast Asian nation of Vietnam where U.S. troops were helping the South Vietnamese in their civil war against the Communist-held North Vietnam. As the war escalated, students and others began to protest the draft and America's involvement in Southeast Asia.

- By the middle of the decade, many blacks were discouraged by the slow pace of change through nonviolence. New leaders advocated Black Power, and in major cities frustration often led to violent confrontations like the 1965 Watts riots. In 1967 alone there were 75 race riots. One of the worst was in Detroit, where 43 people were killed before peace was restored.

- After the assassination of Martin Luther King, Jr., in 1968, race riots broke out in 124 cities.

- Women demanded equal pay for equal work. No longer content to be suburban housewives, they wanted the same career opportunities and choices afforded to men. Betty Friedan led the women's liberation movement and formed the National Organization of Women.

- Migrant workers united under the leadership of Cesar Chavez and protested the unsafe, low-paying conditions of their labor.

- Lyndon Johnson announced that he would not run in the 1968 presidential election.

- Robert F. Kennedy, brother of the late President Kennedy, decided to seek the Democratic Party nomination. After winning the California primary, he was killed by Sirhan Sirhan.

- The Democratic National Convention was marked by violence between antiwar protestors and police. Jerry Rubin's Youth International Party (Yippies) nominated a pig for president. Ultimately, Rubin and seven other radical antiwar leaders were arrested and charged with conspiracy in starting the riots.

- Republican candidate Richard M. Nixon narrowly won the election of 1968. He began his term in office by announcing a plan for Vietnamization of the war and the withdrawal of American forces.

Introducing the Sixties

On this page you will find some interesting ways to introduce the sixties to the students. Keep in mind that these are suggestions only and it is not necessary to use all of them. Your project selections should be based on student needs, interests, and objectives.

1. **Graffiti Board** Attach a large sheet of butcher paper to a classroom wall or long table. Have the students draw pictures and write slogans and words that reflect sixties life. Add to it throughout the unit of studies.

2. **Sing Along** Learn some protest songs which were typical of the sixties, including "Blowin' in the Wind" by Bob Dylan, "We Shall Overcome," and Phil Och's "I Ain't Marching Anymore."

3. **Fashions** Bouffant hairdos, pillbox hats, and miniskirts were all the rage in sixties fashion. Have students find pictures of sixties clothing (an excellent resource is back issues of *Seventeen* magazine).

4. **Artwork** Display artwork that reflects life in the sixties: op art, minimalism, and comic art. Assign students to create their own sixties artwork. For sample projects see page 55.

5. **Be Peaceful** Turn off the classroom lights, burn incense, and listen to soothing music such as sitar instrumentals. Practice a relaxation technique: Breathe in and out slowly and purposefully.

6. **Flower Children** Be flower children for a day. Tell the students to dress in robes or caftans and wear a flower in their hair. Let them paint flowers and other peace symbols on their faces. As a class, make paper flowers to pass out to other classes at lunchtime or before school begins.

7. **Slogan Tees** Brainstorm a list of peace slogans and symbols typical of the sixties. Ask students to bring in old T-shirts. Use marking pens to decorate the shirts with slogans and peace symbols. Wear the shirts all day.

8. **Beatlemania** The Beatles took the world by storm with their new brand of music. Listen to some Beatles songs from one of their early albums such as *Rubber Soul*. Compare it to one of their later albums like *Sergeant Pepper's Lonely Hearts Club Band*. Note the innovative psychedelic sounds of the latter album.

9. **Read Aloud** To set the mood for the era, read aloud the book *Always to Remember* by Brent K. Ashabranner (Dodd, Mead, 1988) to learn the story of how the Vietnam Memorial in Washington, D.C., was built.

10. **Guest Speaker** Call the local VFW for a list of possible guest speakers. Have students prepare questions to ask the speaker about his or her experiences in Vietnam.

11. **Interview** Direct the students to conduct an interview with family members or friends who lived through the Vietnam War years. For sample interview questions, see page 29.

Discussing the Sixties

Create student interest with a lively discussion. Suggested topics and some methods for implementing them follow.

Vietnam The debate over the Vietnam War continued for some twenty-five years after it was over. Form two groups of students. Assign one group to find all the reasons for United States involvement in the war; the other group is to find all the reasons against United States involvement in the war. Let the students present a debate for the rest of the class. Afterwards, open up the floor for class discussion.

What If Write these questions on the board and ask students to write a response to the appropriate one:

 (*Boys*) If you had been drafted in the sixties, would you have served your country in Vietnam?

 (*Girls*) What would you have thought of someone who did not want to serve his country in Vietnam?

Call on students to share their responses with the class.

Lyrics Find the lyrics to a sixties protest song ("We Shall Overcome" or "Blowin' in the Wind," for example) and make a transparency of the page for the overhead projector. Read the words with the class and talk about the message of the song.

Space The space program was at its all-time high during the sixties. On April 12, 1961, Yuri Gagarin of the Soviet Union became the first human in space. A few days later Alan Shepard became the first American in space. The culmination of this space race was the *Apollo 11* mission to the moon. With the class discuss their opinions of space research. Do they think it necessary or very important? What important information have we learned from these space missions? Have the students give some reasons why the space program should be continued today.

Racism The sixties drew attention to the rampant racism that blacks faced in the United States, particularly in the South. Ask the students if they think racism exists in America today. Have them provide examples and be able to defend their answers.

Women's Lib During the sixties women began to voice their dissatisfaction with their roles in society. No longer were they content to stay at home and be housewives. With the class discuss what options are available to women today. Poll the students to find out how many of their mothers work and make a list of their occupations. What conclusions can students draw from this list?

Counterculture Write the following statement on the board for students to read: During the sixties young people began to pursue a lifestyle vastly different from that of their conservative parents. Typically, they rejected the Establishment, the name given to all symbols of authority, especially the government and parents. Have the students compare these sixties sentiments with present-day values. How do they view the government and their parents?

Important Legislation

A number of important pieces of legislation were ratified in the sixties. An outline of some of these measures is provided below.

Peace Corps President Kennedy created the volunteer agency in 1961 to provide help for developing nations worldwide. For more information about the Peace Corps, see page 15.

Twenty-third Amendment Ratified by voters in 1961, this bill granted residents of the District of Columbia the right to vote in Presidential elections and assigned them three electoral votes.

Test Ban Treaty In 1962 the United States and the Soviet Union signed a treaty to stop testing nuclear bombs.

Twenty-fourth Amendment This amendment, approved in 1964, made poll taxes illegal in federal elections. The taxes had been used throughout the South to keep African Americans from voting. Many were too poor to pay the tax.

Civil Rights Act This 1964 act was the most far-reaching civil rights legislation of the twentieth century. It banned discrimination in public places and employment based on race, sex, religion, or national origin.

Economic Opportunity Act Nine hundred forty-seven million dollars in funds was legislated for preschool education and job training under this 1964 act.

Medicare This 1965 program provided for monetary help for all the elderly to pay their medical bills.

Voting Rights Act Under this 1965 law the federal government had the power to prevent unfair practices, such as literacy tests and poll taxes, from restricting voter registration.

Twenty-fifth Amendment This measure, ratified in 1967, outlined what will happen in the event of the president's death or disability while in office. It also outlined the order in which various government officials would become president, e.g. president, vice president, Speaker of the House of Representatives, etc.

Product Safety Enacted in 1967, this law established the National Commission on Product Safety to provide consumer protection. The purpose of the commission was to investigate and to recommend regulations regarding the safety of consumer goods.

Suggested Activities

Impact Are you familiar with any of these legislative measures? Find out which are still in effect today and which have been replaced by updated versions.

Amendments At the end of 1969 there were 25 amendments to the Constitution. Find out how many there are currently. Write brief summaries of each new one.

Presidential Succession Read the Twenty-fifth Amendment to the Constitution. Make a chart of the presidential succession in the event of the president's death or disability while in office. Find out how Ford, and not Spiro Agnew, succeeded to the presidency after Nixon resigned.

1960s Politics and Economics

Listed and described below are some of the most significant political and economic events of the sixties. Further discussions of the topics can be found on the indicated pages.

The Bay of Pigs

In 1959 Fidel Castro led a successful revolution in Cuba and became increasingly friendly with the Soviet Union. Fearing a close Communist neighbor, the Eisenhower administration allowed the CIA to secretly train Cuban exiles. When Eisenhower left office he informed the new president, John Kennedy, of the situation. On April 17, 1961, 1,400 Cubans landed at the Bay of Pigs to lead a revolt against Castro. Their mission failed when promised U.S. air support never arrived.

The Cuban Missile Crisis

In October 1962 a much more serious Soviet Union confrontation occurred. When President Kennedy discovered that the Soviets were building nuclear missile bases in Cuba, he ordered the U.S. Navy to surround Cuba. Kennedy then dared the Soviet premier, Nikita Khrushchev, to run the blockade. Disaster was averted when Khrushchev agreed to remove the missiles. In exchange, the U.S. agreed not to invade Cuba.

Vietnam War

When Kennedy took office the United States was sending aid to South Vietnam. A decision was made to send military advisers to help train the South Vietnamese, and by 1963 the United States was spending one and one half million dollars a day to support the war. After Kennedy's assassination, President Johnson escalated the U.S. operations in Vietnam. See pages 27 to 32 for more about the Vietnam War.

War on Poverty

Despite a thriving economy, not everyone in the United States was affluent. While many Americans enjoyed televisions, cars, bikes, and nice houses, there were those who did not even have enough to eat. Determined to do something about the problem, President Johnson saw to it that a civil rights act was passed. In addition, programs such as Medicare, Medicaid, Operation Headstart, Upward Bound, and Job Corps were instituted.

Civil Rights

Landmark 1950s decisions had paved the way for integration, but the pace was extremely slow. More and more black leaders led marches and demonstrations to obtain the rights which they were being denied. Despite presidential support of civil rights measures, hatred and bigotry continued. Race riots plagued the country. The fight was just beginning. See pages 33 to 35 for more about this topic.

Women's Liberation

During the early sixties women worked quietly in the background to support the civil rights causes and the antiwar protests. They also began to voice their discontent with their roles in society. They began demanding the same freedoms as men—they wanted to be treated as equals. For more about the women's liberation movement, see pages 36 and 37.

The Peace Corps

With the election of John F. Kennedy, a new tide seemed to rise as people eagerly clamored to join the political process. Thousands of Americans wanted to work to help their nation. One proposal was a peace corps. A bill for such a corps had been introduced to Congress in early 1960 but failed. After Kennedy was elected, the organization was officially founded.

What It Is The Peace Corps is a volunteer agency composed of men and women who want to serve as ambassadors of peace. To date, over 100,000 volunteers have served in 91 different countries.

What It Does Peace Corps volunteers perform a variety of skills and services. They teach any number of subjects from reading to beekeeping to sign language, plant trees, help market and sell handicrafts made by villagers, write newsletters, and build ponds to stock with fish.

Qualifications Participants must meet certain qualifications before becoming Peace Corps volunteers. They must be 18 years of age or older, U.S. citizens, in good health, and willing to serve for two years.

Training Volunteers are trained in the local language, beliefs, and customs of their assigned country. In addition, volunteers must respect the culture and traditions of their host country.

Compensation Peace Corps workers are not given a salary. Instead, volunteers receive a readjustment allowance upon completion of their service. Housing, food, travel, and medical expenses are taken care of by the agency.

Hardships Countries served by the Peace Corps are poor and often lack the most basic facilities and amenities that Americans are accustomed to having and using. Most likely there will be no indoor plumbing, no hot baths, and no television for entertainment. There will be no daily phone conversations with friends and family, as calls (if there are phones available) will be very expensive. In addition, participants have to learn another language, leave most of their possessions behind, and possibly live in huts.

Suggested Activities

Slogan Recruitment ads for the Peace Corps state that the Peace Corps is "the toughest job you will ever love." Discuss what this slogan means.

Preparations If you are interested in a possible internship with the Peace Corps, you might want to become an exchange student first. Write a letter requesting information about the student exchange program at this address: President's International Youth Exchange, Pueblo, CO 81009.

Volunteer To get an idea of what working for the Peace Corps might be like, donate your services at a community food bank or volunteer as a Red Cross aide, for example.

Dwight David Eisenhower

34th President, 1953–1961

Vice President: Richard M. Nixon

Born: October 14, 1890, in Denison, Texas

Died: March 28, 1969

Party: Republican

Parents: David Jacob Eisenhower, Ida Elizabeth Stover

First Lady: Mamie Geneva Doud

Children: Dwight, John

Nickname: Ike

Education: Graduate of West Point Academy

Famous Firsts:

Dwight David Eisenhower

- Eisenhower was the first president to have a putting green installed on the White House lawn.
- His 1956 election marked the first time since 1848 that a president had failed to carry at least one house of Congress for his party.
- He was the first president of all 50 states.
- Eisenhower was the first licensed pilot and the first five-star general elected to the office of president.

Achievements:

- Eisenhower made good on a campaign promise and ended the Korean War.
- In 1953 he appointed Earl Warren, considered to be a moderate, as the new chief justice. Warren led a revolution on the Court when he reversed a 1896 separate-but-equal doctrine.
- He went to Korea to revive the stalled peace talks.

Interesting Facts:

- When he was born, Eisenhower's given name was David Dwight. Later, he switched his first and middle names.
- His mother was a pacifist and cried when he decided to attend West Point.
- Eisenhower ranked 65th in his class of 165 at West Point.
- A professional soldier, he helped General MacArthur break up the Bonus March during the thirties.
- He was the only president to have served in both world wars.
- During WWII, Eisenhower served as the supreme Allied commander.
- When Eisenhower was first approached to run for president, he did not have a political party. The Democrats courted him in 1948, but his views were closer to Republican ideas.
- President Eisenhower's favorite sport was golf, and he could often be found on the White House lawn practicing chip shots.
- Eisenhower also enjoyed painting.
- An accomplished cook, vegetable soup and cornmeal pancakes were two of Eisenhower's best dishes.
- Eisenhower was the last president born in the nineteenth century.
- At the time, Eisenhower was the oldest man ever to be president.

John Fitzgerald Kennedy

35th President, 1961–1963

Vice President: Lyndon B. Johnson

Born: May 29, 1917, Brookline, Massachusetts

Died: November 22, 1963

Party: Democratic

Parents: Joseph Patrick Kennedy, Rose Elizabeth Fitzgerald

First Lady: Jacqueline Lee Bouvier

Children: Caroline; John, Jr.; Patrick (died shortly after birth)

Nickname: JFK

Education: Harvard

Famous Firsts:

John Fitzgerald Kennedy

- Kennedy was the first president to be born in the twentieth century.
- He was the youngest man ever elected president and was the first Roman Catholic to hold the office.
- He was the first president to appoint a sibling to a cabinet post; his younger brother Robert (Bobby) was his attorney general.
- Kennedy and Nixon participated in the first televised debates between presidential candidates.

Achievements:

- Kennedy established the Peace Corps in 1961.
- Kennedy served in WWII and was nearly killed when a Japanese destroyer rammed his gunboat, *PT-109*.
- JFK vowed that the United States would land an American on the moon by the end of the decade. To achieve this goal he funded a five-billion-dollar space program. Although Kennedy began plans for a New Frontier, they were accomplished only after his death.
- Included in his plans were stronger civil rights laws, medicare for the elderly, and increased aid for education.

Interesting Facts:

- JFK and each of his eight siblings were given $1 million when they turned 21.
- At 43, Kennedy was the youngest president ever elected, but he was not the youngest president. That distinction is given to Theodore Roosevelt who was 42 when he assumed office after President McKinley was assassinated.
- Kennedy won the 1960 election by a very slim margin—less than 1% of the popular vote—yet he went on to become a very popular president.
- In 1956, Kennedy published *Profiles in Courage*, a look at eight U.S. Senators. The book was awarded the Pulitzer Prize.
- At 29 Kennedy was elected as a Democratic congressional representative from Massachusetts.

Lyndon Baines Johnson

36th President, 1963–1969

Vice President: Hubert H. Humphrey

Born: August 27, 1908, in Stonewall, Texas

Died: January 22, 1973

Party: Democratic

Parents: Sam Ealy Johnson, Jr., Rebekah Baines

First Lady: Claudia (Lady Bird) Alta Taylor

Children: Lynda, Luci

Nickname: LBJ

Education: Southwest Texas State Teachers College

Famous Firsts:

- Johnson was the first vice-president to witness the assassination of the president whom he succeeded.

- He was the first president to be sworn in by a woman.

Lyndon Baines Johnson

Achievements:

- At 46, Johnson became the Senate Majority Leader in 1955.

- During his administration, more civil rights legislation was passed than under any president in U.S. history.

- In his 1964 State of the Union address, Johnson declared a "War on Poverty."

- His Great Society established Medicare and Medicaid.

- He passed the Civil Rights Act of 1964.

- Johnson established the Head Start and Job Corps programs.

- His Voting Rights Act of 1965 outlawed literacy tests used to keep African Americans from registering to vote.

- Immigration quota laws were changed for the first time since the 1920s.

Interesting Facts:

- Johnson spent one year teaching school before he entered politics.

- LBJ proposed to his wife the day after they first met; the couple married two months later.

- In a surprise move, Johnson announced he would not run for re-election in 1968.

Richard Milhous Nixon

37th President, 1969–1974

Vice Presidents: Spiro T. Agnew, Gerald R. Ford

Born: January 9, 1913, in Yorba Linda, California

Died: April 22, 1994

Party: Republican

Parents: Francis Anthony Nixon, Hannah Milhous

First Lady: Thelma Patricia (Pat) Catherine Ryan

Children: Patricia, Julie

Nickname: Tricky Dick

Education: Duke University School of Law (ranked third in his class)

Famous Firsts:

- Nixon was the first president to resign from office.
- He was the first president to visit China.

Richard Milhous Nixon

Achievements:

- Nixon worked as a lawyer until 1946 when he won election to Congress.
- During his first year as president, the United States won the space race when *Apollo 11* astronaut Neil Armstrong became the first person to walk on the moon.
- Nixon proposed to end the Vietnam War with Vietnamization (replacing American troops with South Vietnamese soldiers). During the Vietnamization process, Nixon ordered an increase in the bombing of North Vietnam. In fact, more bomb tonnage was dropped on North Vietnam in this short period than on Germany, Italy, and Japan combined during all of WWII.
- On June 8, 1969, President Nixon announced that 25,000 U.S. soldiers would leave Vietnam by the end of August and 35,000 more by September 16.

Interesting Facts:

- Nixon was often accused of being paranoid. For example, he ordered his staff to keep a list of his enemies, from politicians to businesspersons, athletes, and movie stars.
- Richard Nixon was born in a house built by his father.
- In 1968 Nixon's daughter, Julie, married David Eisenhower, grandson of former President Eisenhower.

Presidential Quotes

Three presidents were inaugurated during the sixties, and during their terms in office each said words that are still considered important. Read each quote below. On the lines that follow, explain what each one means.

President John Fitzgerald Kennedy

"And so, my fellow Americans, ask not what your country can do for you; ask what you can do for your country. My fellow citizens of the world, ask not what America will do for you, but what together we can do for the freedom of man."–*Inaugural Address, January 20, 1961*

_____

_____

_____

_____

_____

President Lyndon Baines Johnson

"This administration today, here and now, declares unconditional war on poverty in America . . . . It will not be a short or easy struggle, no single weapon or strategy will suffice, but we shall not rest until that war is won."–*State of the Union message, January 8, 1964*

_____

_____

_____

_____

_____

President Richard Milhous Nixon

"We have found ourselves rich in goods, but ragged in spirit; reaching with magnificent precision for the moon but falling into raucous discord on earth. We are caught in war, wanting peace. We are torn by divisions, wanting unity."–*First Inaugural Address, January 20, 1969*

_____

_____

_____

_____

_____

20

Just Like Lincoln

After the 1963 assassination of President Kennedy, some historians began to note some uncanny similarities between his death and that of President Lincoln. For example, both had been shot in the head by an assassin, and at his widow's request, Kennedy's funeral was modeled after Lincoln's.

Let students find out more likenesses between the two with this game. Make a copy of this page for each pair of students. Direct them to cut apart the cards and match the answers to the correct questions. Review the questions and answers in whole group.

1. What do both presidents' last names have in common?	a. They are full of inconsistencies.
2. How well-liked were both presidents?	b. Both inherited a wartime dispute.
3. What is believed about the official reports about the two assassinations?	c. Both were from the South–Lyndon from Texas, Andrew from Tennessee.
4. What same last name did the two vice presidents share?	d. Both contain seven letters.
5. What happened to both assassins before they could be brought to trial?	e. Days after the assassinations, both were shot and killed.
6. What role did war play in their administrations?	f. Lincoln and Kennedy were popular with the people but both had enemies.
7. What two things are the same about the names of the presidents' assassins?	g. Both had three names containing a total of 15 letters.
8. From which area of the United States did both Johnsons originate?	h. Their last name was Johnson (Andrew and Lyndon Baines).

Four First Ladies

Mamie Eisenhower, Jacqueline Kennedy, Lady Bird Johnson, and Pat Nixon were all first ladies during the sixties. Each brought a distinct style and different personality to the role. Research and find out the contributions of each first lady during her time in office. Write each of the following phrases in the correct section on the chart below.

- supported the cause of volunteerism
- bouffant hairdos and pillbox hats
- beautifying America's landscape
- proud to be a housewife
- historically correct renovation of the White House
- daughters were Lynda and Luci
- served the longest as First Lady
- The Highway Beautification Act
- one of the youngest First Ladies ever

- the first president's wife to travel to Africa
- known for her trademark pink
- traveled to support the Great Society programs
- daughters were Julie and Tricia
- greeted tourists visiting the White House
- led the nation with grace and courage after her husband's death
- nurtured her husband during his frequent illnesses

Mamie

_____

Lady Bird

_____

Jackie

_____

Pat

_____

22

A Look Back at Jackie

There has never been a First Lady quite like Jacqueline Bouvier Kennedy. She was young, beautiful, and vibrant and added a touch of elegance lacking in the previous older administration. Her hair and clothing styles were simple yet graceful and widely copied by American women. The Jackie look was the fashionable way to dress. When her husband died in office, Jacqueline Kennedy stoically led the country in mourning. She was a special woman, just right for the times.

Jacqueline Kennedy

Jacqueline Lee Bouvier, or Jackie as the world called her, was born on July 28, 1929, in East Hampton on Long Island. Her father was John Vernon Bouvier III, a rich and handsome New York stockbroker; her mother, Janet Lee Bouvier, was a beautiful woman who was also a skilled horsewoman. Jackie Bouvier and her younger sister, Lee, were treated like princesses by their parents and the family's many servants. Even her parents' divorce when she was eight did not diminish her standing in society, and she continued to attend private schools. When she was 13, her mother married a rich man, Hugh Auchincloss. Throughout these times Jackie Bouvier kept up with her favorite sport of horseback riding, even boarding her mare, Danseuse, in a nearby stable while attending Miss Porter's School for Young Women.

In 1946 Jackie Bouvier had her debutante party and was named Queen Deb of the Year by the local press. The social scene failed to impress her, and she entered college that fall. After completing her studies at George Washington University, she got a job at the *Washington Times-Herald* as an inquiring camera girl. Through some friends, she met the most eligible bachelor in Washington, John F. Kennedy. The two were married on September 12, 1953, with 1,700 invited guests from high society and politics.

Jacqueline Bouvier Kennedy quit her job and played the part of perfect political wife. She had three children, Caroline, John F. Kennedy, Jr., and Patrick, who died shortly after birth. When the young family moved into the White House, a transformation seemed to take place. Jackie Kennedy was just 31 and her husband, at 43, was the youngest man ever elected to the presidency. It was, as some called it, Camelot.

During her years as First Lady, Jacqueline Kennedy renovated and restored the White House to reflect its historical past and took the entire nation on a televised tour into the White House on February 14, 1962. She supported a number of cultural and artistic endeavors and raised the level of official entertaining by inviting America's best artists to perform at the White House.

After the death of her husband, Jacqueline Kennedy went on to remarry and then to build a powerful career in the publishing world. She fought to maintain her privacy, both for herself and her children, after the White House years. For many years, she was among the most admired women in the world and until her death on May 19, 1994, one of the most photographed.

Suggested Activity

Completion Research and find out how Jacqueline Kennedy spent the remainder of her years after the White House.

Election Facts and Figures

	Election of 1960	Election of 1964	Election of 1968
Democrats	John F. Kennedy, a senator from Massachusetts, was nominated for president and selected Texas senator Lyndon Baines Johnson as his running mate.	President Lyndon Baines Johnson received the presidential nomination with Minnesota senator Hubert H. Humphrey for vice president.	At a convention marked by protests and violence, Vice President Hubert Humphrey became the presidential candidate with Senator Edmund Muskie of Maine as his running mate.
Republicans	Vice-President Richard M. Nixon ran for president with Henry Cabot Lodge, the U.S. ambassador to the UN, as his vice president.	Barry Goldwater, a conservative senator from Arizona, ran for president with William Miller of New York for vice president.	Former Vice President Richard M. Nixon was paired with Maryland governor Spiro T. Agnew for vice president.
Other			George C. Wallace, former governor of Alabama, broke with the Democrats to form the American Independent Party and ran for president with General Curtis LeMay for vice president.
Issues	Both candidates had similar political ideas. They believed in a strong military that could protect the United States from a Communist attack and supported funding for welfare programs for the poor.	Goldwater's brand of politics scared many Americans. He opposed civil rights legislation, wanted to make Social Security voluntary, and proposed deep cuts in social programs.	Vietnam remained the big issue in this election. Humphrey found it difficult to distance himself from Johnson, to whom he had remained loyal. Nixon talked vaguely about a secret plan to end the war. Wallace campaigned for strict law and order.
Slogans	Kennedy promised to lead Americans to a New Frontier.	Johnson's slogan was "All the way with LBJ"; Goldwater's slogan was "In your heart, you know he's right."	
Results	John F. Kennedy won by a narrow margin—electoral votes, 303 (Kennedy) to 219 (Nixon). Senator Harry F. Byrd received 15 electoral votes.	Johnson won by an overwhelming majority—electoral votes, 486 (Johnson) to 52 (Goldwater).	Nixon received less than 51 percent of the popular vote. The electoral vote was 301 (Nixon) to 191 (Humphrey). Wallace received 45 electoral votes, the strongest third party finish since Theodore Roosevelt in 1912.

　　　24

More About the Elections

Here are some ways to use the Election Facts and Figures on page 24. Select those activities and projects which best suit your classroom needs.

1. Prepare a classroom chart with four different sections, each marked with a different vice presidential candidate's name. Pair the students. Then make several copies of page 24. Cut apart the boxes and randomly give one to each pair of students. Instruct the pairs to complete the following activity. Find out more about the men nominated for vice president—where they were born, their childhood and schooling, their political backgrounds, where they are now, etc. Compile all the information gathered onto your prepared chart.

2. Kennedy narrowly won his bid for the presidency, and many critics maintain that it was due to the four televised debates he had with Republican candidate Richard Nixon. Research and find out the factors which gave Kennedy the advantage in these debates and helped him win the election.

3. In 1960 Senator Harry F. Byrd received 15 electoral votes although he did not run for office and received no popular votes. Discuss some possible reasons for this. Have the students research the electoral college system and take sides in a debate over this system of electing a president.

4. In 1964 Senator Barry Goldwater was nominated as the Republican presidential candidate. An extreme conservative, his views frightened many Americans. Probably his statements about nuclear war hurt him the most in this campaign. Direct the students to learn more about this man and to find answers to the following: Exactly what were Goldwater's views on nuclear war? How did the Johnson campaign play on these views with a TV commercial?

5. All four men who were president during the sixties faced the Vietnam problem. Group the students and have them make a time line or a flow chart to show changes in the levels of United States troops and arms during the sixties.

6. Compare the four 1960s presidents in the matter of legislation for civil rights. Who did the most for civil rights? Who did the least? What were some of the civil rights laws passed during the sixties? Group the students and have them prepare a chronological list of these laws and what each provided.

7. Extend the information provided on page 24 with some other facts and figures. For example, find out how many popular votes the candidates garnered in their respective elections. Make a chart comparing the figures. See page 26 for some math problems using these figures.

8. Discuss with the students what history now has to say about each of the sixties presidents. (They may have to research which president during this era is considered the greatest leader or the greatest supporter of civil rights, for example.) Have each student rank the presidents from most effective to least effective. Let them defend their choices.

9. Compose math word problems using the information about electoral votes found on page 26.

Election Math

In the chart below you will find the number of electoral votes and popular votes for each presidential election during the sixties. Use this chart to answer the questions that follow. Show your work in the space provided.

		Electoral Vote	Popular Vote
1960	Kennedy	303	34,221,344
	Nixon	219	34,106,671
	Byrd	15	0
1964	Johnson	486	43,126,584
	Goldwater	52	27,177,838
1968	Nixon	301	31,785,148
	Humphrey	191	31,274,503
	Wallace	46	9,901,151

1. How many more electoral votes were there in 1968 than in 1960? _____

_____

2. How many popular votes were there altogether in 1964? How many total electoral votes that year?_____

_____

3. What is the difference between the number of popular votes gathered by the winners of the 1964 and the 1968 elections? _____

_____

4. How many popular votes were netted altogether by the four unsuccessful candidates in each election?_____

_____

5. How many popular votes were cast altogether in the 1968 presidential election? _____

_____

6. How many more popular votes did Kennedy get than Nixon? _____

_____

Events in Vietnam

The Vietnam War was the costliest and longest war fought in U.S. history. More bomb tonnage was dropped on North Vietnam than on Germany, Italy, and Japan during all of World War II. Over 50,000 American troops died in Vietnam. How did the United States become involved in the war and what was the outcome? These and other issues are addressed in the various sections below.

Beginnings During WWII, Japan invaded French Indochina. After the war, the communist Vietminh seized the capital city, Hanoi, and declared the Democratic Republic of Vietnam or North Vietnam. France supported Emperor Bao Dai and helped to establish a new state of Vietnam, or South Vietnam, with a capital at Saigon. The United States recognized the Saigon government. Meanwhile, the French and the Vietminh were at war. In 1954, at the battle of Dien Bien Phu, the French suffered defeat and withdrew their forces. Under accords drawn at a meeting in Geneva, France and North Vietnam agreed to a truce and future free elections for reunification. Neither side honored the accords, however, and civil war continued. In 1954 the U.S. offered direct economic aid to South Vietnam. The following year U.S. military advisers were sent to train Vietnamese soldiers.

Domino Theory When Kennedy came into office, his predecessor, President Eisenhower, warned him that if the U.S. allowed South Vietnam to fall to the Communists, the next in line would be Laos, Cambodia, Burma, and on into the Subcontinent. This Domino Theory worried Kennedy, and he pledged to help South Vietnam remain independent. U.S. economic and military aid increased. In 1961, 400 army personnel were sent to Saigon to operate two noncombat helicopter units. By 1962 more than 10,000 U.S. military men were in place.

Gulf of Tonkin After President Kennedy was assassinated, President Johnson vowed not to lose Vietnam to communism. On August 2, 1964, it was reported that the *USNS Maddox*, a U.S. destroyer in the Gulf of Tonkin, had been attacked by North Vietnam. This incident led Congress to pass a resolution allowing the president to use U.S. troops without a formal declaration of war or approval from Congress. The president ordered jets to begin retaliatory bombing of military targets in North Vietnam. In March of 1965, the first ground-force combat units of marines brought the level of U.S. troops to 27,000. By the end of the year there were almost 200,000 American combat forces in Vietnam.

Tet Offensive North Vietnam and its Viet Cong allies launched a huge surprise attack on major cities in the South on January 30, 1968. Because it began during Tet, the Vietnamese New Year, the attack was called the Tet Offensive. The U.S. counterattack was successful, but both sides suffered massive casualties.

Peace Talks Following the Tet Offensive the United States halted bombing in Vietnam, and peace talks were initiated in Paris. No agreement could be reached at that time. Early in 1969 President Nixon announced his plan for Vietnamization of the war, and for a gradual withdrawal of U.S. forces. By September of 1969, 55,000 American soldiers had left Vietnam. Secret peace talks between Henry Kissinger of the U.S. and Le Duc Tho of North Vietnam began in Paris in 1970. The talks continued for three years, as did the fighting in Vietnam. Finally, in January of 1973, a cease fire agreement was reached. The U.S. and its allies withdrew from Vietnam in March of that year.

Suggested Activity

Research Find out more about the following people, places, and events associated with the Vietnam war.

My Lai Massacre	Haiphong Harbor	POWs
Lt. Calley	Ho Chi Minh Trail	The fall of Saigon
General Wiliam Westmoreland	Laos	Allies of the U.S.
Danang	Cambodia	Allies of North Vietnam

Mapping the Terrain

The terrain and climate of Vietnam was unfamiliar territory to most American soldiers. After all, Vietnam was mostly jungle with thick growths of shrubs and trees. Conditions there were unlike any other ever encountered by the military. Learn more about Vietnam with this mapping activity. Read the story and write the names of the locations on the lines provided.

After the Vietcong defeated combat regiments in May and June of 1965, the government of 1._____collapsed. The United States began pouring in more troops and continued bombing 2._____. Supported by the Soviet Union and 3._____, guerilla forces multiplied. Reinforcements and munitions were smuggled along the 4._____through 5._____and 6._____into South Vietnam. By mid-1967, there were no signs of the war ending. All U.S. strategy had failed, and American combat casualties rose dramatically. On January 31, 1968, the communists launched surprise attacks on every major South Vietnamese village and city. At 7._____, American soldiers found mass graves of people killed by the Vietcong. The Vietcong eventually withdrew from Hue, but fighting for 8._____raged on for 75 days. By the time the offensive had been defeated in March, the United States counted 2,000 soldiers dead, the South Vietnamese 4,000, and the North Vietnamese 40,000. Still, the fighting continued.

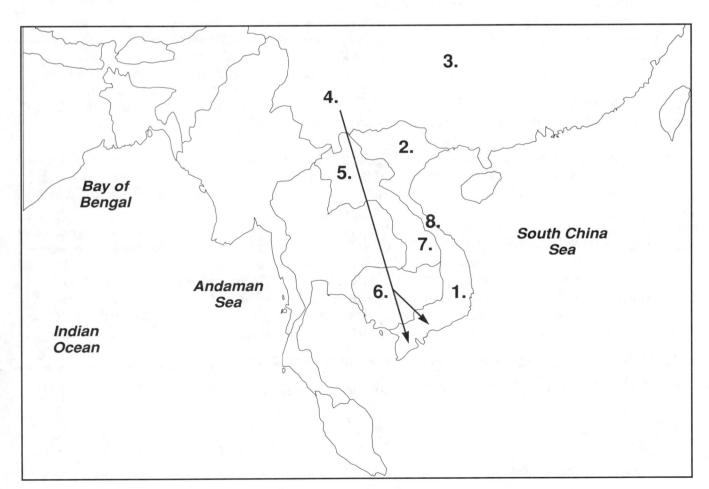

28

A Vietnam Interview

Interview an individual who was a teenager or adult during the Vietnam War.

Name _____

Age_____

Occupation _____

1. What do you know about the Vietnam War?_____

   _____

2. What were you doing during the Vietnam War? _____

   _____

3. Did you or anyone else you know serve in Vietnam?_____

   _____

4. If you did not serve in Vietnam, how did you feel about those who did? _____

   _____

5. Did you know anyone who evaded the draft? _____

   _____

6. How did you feel about draft evaders? _____

   _____

7. Did you ever protest against the war in Vietnam? Why or why not? _____

   _____

8. Do you think the United States should have become involved in Vietnam?_____

   _____

9. Have your views changed since the war ended? If so, how?_____

   _____

10. If the United States became involved in a war today, would you serve in the armed forces?
    Defend your response. _____

    _____

    _____

    _____

POW Code

About 700 Americans were captured and held prisoners near Hanoi during the Vietnam War. Conditions in these prisons were deplorable, and the prisoners themselves were treated brutally. Often, the soldiers were kept in separate cells. In order to keep their spirits up, the POWs developed a special code which they tapped out on the cell walls. Use the chart below to figure out the message that this POW might have wanted to send the American people to tell them about his treatment.

Hint: In the chart, 1–1 stands for A, 1–3 for C; M is 3–2, U is 4–5, and K is 2–6.

1	2	3	4	5
1–A	1–F	1–L	1–Q	1–V
2–B	2–G	2–M	2–R	2–W
3–C	3–H	3–N	3–S	3–X
4–D	4–I	4–O	4–T	4–Y
5–E	5–J	5–P	5–U	5–Z
	6–K			

___ ___ ___ ___ ___ ___ ___ ___ ___ ___ ___ ___ ___ ___ ___.
3–2 5–4 1–2 1–5 1–4 2–4 4–3 1–3 3–4 3–3 1–3 4–2 1–5 4–4 1–5

___ ___ ___ ___ ___ ___ ___ ___ ___ ___ ___ ___ ___ ___ ___ ___
2–4 2–3 1–1 5–1 1–5 1–1 1–2 4–5 1–3 2–6 1–5 4–4 2–1 3–4 4–2 1–1

___ ___ ___ ___ ___ ___ ___. ___ ___ ___ ___ ___ ___ ___ ___
4–4 3–4 2–4 3–1 1–5 4–4 2–4 1–1 3–2 1–2 1–5 2–4 3–3 2–2 4–4 3–4

___ ___ ___ ___ ___ ___ ___ ___ ___ ___ ___ ___ ___ ___ ___ ___
4–2 4–4 4–5 4–2 1–5 1–4 1–2 3–4 4–4 2–3 3–2 1–5 3–3 4–4 1–1 3–1

___ ___ ___ ___ ___ ___ ___ ___ ___ ___ ___ ___ ___ ___ ___.
3–1 5–4 1–1 3–3 1–4 3–5 2–3 5–4 4–3 2–4 1–3 1–1 3–1 3–1 5–4

Vietnam Stats

Until the Tet Offensive in 1968, the majority of the American people had supported the war in Vietnam. The staggering statistics about the wounded and dead, however, shocked everyone. It was one of the reasons that so many people began calling for an end to the war. Examine the statistics in the box below and answer the questions that follow.

Year	American Troops in Vietnam	American Deaths in Vietnam
1965	180,000	1,728
1966	380,000	6,053
1967	450,000	11,058
1968	540,000	17,622
1969	543,000	11,527
1970	280,000	6,065
1971	140,000	2,348
1972	70,000	561

1. In which year were the most American troops in Vietnam? _____

2. In which year were the fewest American troops in Vietnam? _____

3. What is the difference between the figures from question one and question two above? _____

4. In which year did the casualty figures peak? _____

5. In which years was the death toll more than 11,000? _____ _____ _____

6. What is the difference between the number of deaths in 1965 and the number of deaths in 1972? _____

7. What is the total number of American deaths in Vietnam for 1965 to 1969? _____

8. What is the number of American troops who served in Vietnam from 1965 to 1972? _____

9. Of the troops in Vietnam in 1966, approximately what percentage died? _____

10. Of the troops in Vietnam in 1968, approximately what percentage died? _____

"Hell No, We Won't Go"

Read the following paragraphs about the draft. Answer the questions that follow. Use the back of this page, if necessary.

When two batallions of Marines were sent to guard the Da Nang air base on March 8, 1965, there were already some 20,000 American troops in Vietnam. By the end of the year, the number had reached 200,000. In order to provide ever-increasing numbers of troops, the army used the draft to force men into military service. Not everyone supported the draft, however. The prospect of dying in a combat zone was very real. Demonstrations and antiwar rallies were held on college campuses across the nation. "Hell no, we won't go," became a national anthem among protestors. Students were required to register for the draft. If they attended school, they automatically received a deferment or postponement of their service. Some young men burned their registration cards, an act that was against the law. An estimated 250,000 avoided registration. Many of them fled to Canada and Europe where they participated in huge demonstrations against U.S. involvement in Vietnam. They remained outside the United States until President Carter pardoned them in 1977.

Questions

1. Was the draft fair? Why or why not? Defend your answer. _____

   _____

   _____

   _____

2. The draft did not apply to women. Should women be exempt from the draft?_____

   Explain your answer. _____

   _____

   _____

3. How were the problems of this draft similar to the draft during the Civil War?

   _____

   _____

   _____

   _____

The Civil Rights Movement

Civil rights had long been an issue, but not until the sixties did it reach such urgency. Tired of the slow pace of legislative changes, African American leaders emerged and pushed the civil rights movement to the forefront. Listed below are some important 1960s developments in the civil rights cause.

Sit-Ins This nonviolent action was started on February 1, 1960, by a group of four black students who had gone to the Woolworth's store in Greensboro, North Carolina, to buy supplies. When they sat at the lunch counter for coffee, they were told they could not be served. In protest, the group remained seated until the store closed.

Freedom Rides This project protested the segregation of long-distance interstate bus travel. In 1961 a group called CORE (see page 34) announced plans for seven blacks and six whites to begin a Freedom Ride from Washington, D.C., to New Orleans, Louisiana. The bus did not get far before there was trouble. Angry whites beat several riders and set fire to the bus. Nevertheless, several more freedom rides were planned and carried out before the U.S. government initiated very clear rules about integrating bus stations.

March on Washington On August 28, 1963, more than 2,000 buses and 30 special trains had brought a quarter of a million people to Washington, D.C., to protest against discrimination. People of all races and from all over the country traveled to our nation's capital so their voices could be heard. This is where Martin Luther King, Jr., delivered his famous "I Have a Dream . . ." speech.

Mississippi Freedom Summer During the summer of 1964, close to 1,000 students from the North traveled to Mississippi to participate in the Mississippi Summer Project. Bob Moses had planned the event to create a new political party and provide volunteers to register black voters. This angered many whites, and on June 21, three young civil rights workers were killed.

Selma to Montgomery March On March 21, 1965, Dr. Martin Luther King, Jr., lead a group of 4,000 people across the Edmund Pettus Bridge. By the time they reached Montgomery on March 25, they numbered 25,000.

Poor People's Campaign This was Dr. Martin Luther King, Jr.'s, last campaign. In 1968 he had decided to take his cause North to work to eliminate poverty among blacks and whites.

Riots In Los Angeles from August 11–16, 1965, race riots spread throughout the city's Watts area, sparked by charges of police brutality. National Guardsmen were called in to restore order. During one week in July of 1967, 75 race riots erupted in Detroit. Forty-three people died in the conflicts.

Suggested Activities

Changes Discuss what important changes were brought about by the civil rights movement and how the U.S. government helped the cause.

Resource For more information about these issues read . . . *If You Lived at the Time of Martin Luther King, Jr.,* by Ellen Levine (Scholastic, Inc., 1990).

Leading the Cause

Not everyone agreed with Martin Luther King, Jr.'s ideas. Although the civil rights groups and black leaders believed that blacks and whites must be treated equally, their methods were not all the same. Read about some of these groups and leaders of the civil rights cause.

NAACP The oldest civil rights group, the National Association for the Advancement of Colored People, was founded in 1909. Its members believed that the best way to change bad laws was through the court system. Lawyers for the NAACP argued that segregation was wrong, and they won several important cases.

CORE The Congress of Racial Equality was founded in Chicago in 1942. Composed of black and white members, they believed in nonviolent direct action and organized the Freedom Rides of 1961.

SNCC Founded in 1960 by students from the sit-ins, the Student Nonviolent Coordinating Committee helped African Americans to register to vote.

SCLC The Southern Christian Leadership Conference was founded by Ralph Abernathy and Martin Luther King, Jr., following the bus boycott in Montgomery, Alabama. See page 35 for more about King's life.

Malcolm X Malcolm X was originally a leader of the Nation of Islam, or Black Muslims. He spoke out against integration and believed that blacks and whites should not live together. After a trip to Mecca in Saudi Arabia, he changed his ideas about hate and violence. Malcolm broke with the Black Muslims to form his own group. In 1964 he was killed by some men in the Muslim group.

Malcolm X

Stokely Carmichael

Medgar Evers As Mississippi field secretary of the NAACP, he coordinated the effort to desegregate public facilities in Jackson, Mississippi. His assassination on June 13, 1963, led President Kennedy to advocate a new, comprehensive civil rights program.

Huey Newton In 1966 Huey Newton and other black activists founded the Black Panther Party, the original purpose of which was to protect African American neighborhoods from police brutality.

Stokely Carmichael When Stokely Carmichael was elected president of the SNCC, he decided to take the organization in a more aggressive direction. He talked about change by any means necessary and black power. In 1966 SNCC expelled all whites from its organization.

Suggested Activities

Nation of Islam Louis Farrakhan became an outspoken leader of the Nation of Islam later in the century. Find out his views on civil rights, whites, and integration.

Assassins Medgar Evers' assassins were not brought to trial until some thirty years after the event. Find out why it took so long to prosecute his killers.

Update Find out about current changes in the NAACP. Who is the current leader and how is the organization affecting social change?

Martin Luther King, Jr.

On April 4, 1968, the world lost one of its greatest heroes of social causes, Martin Luther King, Jr. He was a man who devoted his life to the nonviolent promotion of civil rights, yet he died a violent death.

Martin Luther King, Jr.

King was born in Atlanta, Georgia, on January 15, 1929. His mother was a teacher and his father was a minister. An excellent student, King graduated from high school at the age of 15. He continued his education at Morehouse College and went on to study theology at Crozer Theological Seminar in Chester, Pennsylvania. King later attended Boston University and received his Ph.D. in 1955. While he was in Boston, he met Coretta Scott and they married on June 18, 1953.

For five years during the fifties, King was pastor of Dexter Avenue Baptist Church in Montgomery, Alabama, but he resigned so that he could devote all his time to the civil rights cause. He began to speak out against the discrimination that African Americans were facing. African Americans attended separate and unequal schools, they were forced to sit in the back of buses, and they could not eat at the same lunch counter as whites. It was degrading and unfair, and King was not afraid to speak out about these injustices. After African American Rosa Parks refused to give up her bus seat to a white man, King helped organize the Montgomery bus boycott. King was arrested and jailed, his home was bombed, and threats were made against his life, but he continued his nonviolent protest. As a result, the city changed its segregation laws.

As a student, King had learned about Mohandas Gandhi's technique of nonviolent persuasion for social protest. During a trip to India in 1959, King was able to enhance his knowledge of Gandhi's principles. These were the cornerstone of King's protest.

On August 28, 1963, King led the March on Washington. A quarter of a million people of all races from all over the country traveled to Washington, D.C., to protest discrimination. This demonstration led to the passage of the 1964 Civil Rights Act and the 1965 Voting Rights Act. A charismatic leader and an excellent orator, Martin Luther King, Jr., urged his followers to employ civil disobedience and nonviolent methods of protest. In 1964 he was awarded the Nobel Peace Prize for his work. It was a fitting tribute to a true hero of the times.

Suggested Activities

Speech Martin Luther King, Jr., was a powerful speaker and is probably best known for his "I Have a Dream . . ." speech. Read the complete text of the speech and to write a summary of the important ideas.

Comparisons Compare the lives and works of Medgar Evers and Malcolm X with those of Martin Luther King, Jr. Construct a chart or three-way Venn diagram. Alternatively, you can compare King's methods of nonviolence with those of Mohandas Gandhi.

Background You may be interested to learn what sparked King's dream of equality. Read "Does Friendship Have a Color?" by Valerie Wilson Wesley from the January/February 1996 issue of *Creative Classroom*. Related activities accompany the story.

Women's Liberation

In the years leading up to the 1960s, the usual role of women in American society was that of the traditional housewife and stay-at-home mother. Several television programs reflected these views. *I Love Lucy*, *Ozzie and Harriet*, and *Leave It to Beaver*, for example, depicted happy households where Mom was content to take care of her family. Writer Betty Friedan questioned this traditionalist view of women, and during the early sixties she investigated women's true feelings. Friedan found that many of them were unhappy and dissatisfied with the limitations of being housewives. As these women began seeking ways to change their lives, the women's liberation movement gathered momentum.

Betty Friedan

Born Betty Goldstein in Peoria, Illinois, to a wealthy family, she was a bright, outgoing child. After graduating from high school as valedictorian, she went on to study psychology at Smith College. There she became editor of the college newspaper. This experience helped her in her job as a labor journalist. However, it did not prepare her for the discrimination she and other women faced in the work force. Her marriage and motherhood only reinforced the limited roles available to women in the sixties. Then she was asked to conduct a poll of her college classmates about their life experiences. Friedan was amazed to find that the 200 women who responded were as dissatisfied with their places in society as she was. Friedan wrote an article about her survey results, but no magazine would publish it. One publisher, however, was interested in a book. After five years of interviews and researching, *The Feminine Mystique* was published in 1963. Enormously popular, the book pointed out that American females received educations that opened their minds yet left them facing closed doors to all but a few career choices. As more and more women were drawn to feminism, Friedan founded a group in 1966 called NOW, the National Organization of Women. NOW worked to achieve equal rights for women and is still an active force in society and politics. Betty Friedan served as its president until 1970 and today continues to promote women's equality.

Suggested Activity

Discuss What are women's roles in society today? Do women have equal rights? Are they paid the same as men for equal work? Are the same career opportunities available to women as to men?

The Problem In *The Feminine Mystique*, Betty Friedan called it "the problem that has no name." Identify and discuss the problem. Does it still exist?

Excerpts Read excerpts from *The Feminine Mystique*. Discuss the content.

A Congresswoman

In 1968 Shirley Chisholm was elected to the United States House of Representatives. Although she was not the first woman to serve in the United States Congress, she was the first African American woman to hold such a position.

Shirley Chisholm

Shirley Anita St. Hill was born on November 30, 1924, in Brooklyn, New York. She and her three younger sisters spent several years in Barbados, where they lived on their grandmother's farm. Shirley St. Hill returned to Brooklyn at the age of 11. She excelled in school, graduating from a girls' high school there and receiving a degree in sociology from Brooklyn College. Later, she earned her master's degree in elementary education at Columbia University. Throughout her school years, she worked on the campaigns of female students running for office. Shirley St. Hill married Conrad Chisholm in 1949. She taught school and became the director of Brooklyn's Friends Day Nursery. In 1959 she was an educational consultant in the day-care division of New York City's Bureau of Child Welfare. When she heard a white politician make unflattering comments about black leadership, she decided to prove that African Americans were capable of being leaders. In 1964 she entered politics and was the first black woman from Brooklyn elected to the New York State Assembly. Elected to the United States Congress in 1968, Chisholm served for seven terms. She advocated women's rights, abortion reform, day care, environmental protection, job training, and an end to United States' involvement in Vietnam. She also opposed the seniority system in Congress. In 1972 Chisholm ran unsuccessfully for the presidential nomination. She continued in Congress until 1982, when she declined to run for an eighth term.

Chisholm became a professor at Mount Holyoke College in Massachusetts.

Suggested Activities

Figures How does your state measure up? Find out if any women currently hold elected offices at the city, state, and national levels.

Women in the House Make a list of women who are presently serving in the House of Representatives and Senate and which states they represent. Add to the list any women who currently hold positions in the president's cabinet.

ERA Define the Equal Rights Amendment. Find out the fate of the Amendment and how many states actually ratified it.

Slogans Shirley Chisholm's campaign slogan in 1968 was "Unbought and Unbossed." In 1970, she published a book with the same title. What do you think this slogan meant to Chisholm? Write slogans you might use to represent yourself in an election.

The Counterculture

By the mid-1960s, there were more young adults, ages 18–20, than ever before. Many followed the traditional patterns and lifestyle, but others resisted the pressure to conform that had marked the fifties and rebelled against the "Establishment." Called "hippies", these young people formed a counterculture based on earlier Bohemian groups like the beatniks of the fifties. Encouraged to "turn on, tune in, and drop out," they hoped to form a utopian community. In 1966 over 15,000 hippies lived in the Haight-Ashbury district of San Francisco.

Fashions Hippies adopted a wide range of clothing intended to express their individuality. They wore a variety of styles and used a variety of fabrics in their clothing, often bought from thrift stores. Both men and women had long hair, and the men often had beards. "Love beads" and flower motifs were popular decorations for clothing. Later, bell-bottomed pants and T-shirts tie-dyed in bright psychedelic colors became popular.

Lifestyle Hippies rejected the traditional family structure and often lived in groups called "communes", where everything was freely shared. The goal was to make these communes self-sufficient. Because they wanted to live in the present, their philosophy was to "go with the flow," and "hang loose." In their quest to expand their consciousness, hippies often experimented with hallucinogenic drugs like LSD. Their psychedelic drug experiences led many to mysticism and Oriental philosophies like Zen and Tibetan Buddhism and yoga. The Maharishi Mahesh Yogi attracted many followers, including the Beatles, with his Transcendental Meditation techniques. Others turned to astrology and tarot.

Politics Members of the counterculture felt that they had been betrayed by political leaders. They took part in demonstrations against social injustice, racial segregation, and the Vietnam War, urging others to "Give peace a chance" and "Make love not war."

Summer of Love In 1967 hippies gathered in San Francisco for an event called the Gathering of the Tribes for the Human Be-in, popularly known as the Summer of Love. More than 50,000 young people assembled in the Haight-Ashbury district for this event. In October of that year, a hippie death service was held, and leaders urged the assembled hippies to take their message to the world.

A campus group called Students for a Democratic Society (SDS) inspired students to take political action. This movement became known as the "New Left" and allied itself with other radical organizations like the Black Panthers. The satirical Yippies (Youth International Party) sought personal and social liberation. They became visible with their demonstrations for civil rights and against the Vietnam War. In 1968 several leaders of the New Left were arrested and tried after a violent confrontation at the Democratic National Convention.

Suggested Activities

Protest Hippies demonstrated for a number of social causes. Brainstorm a list of current topical causes. Form small groups and select a cause. Write slogans, make posters, and present a demonstration for your cause.

Where Are They Now? Generate a list of people associated with the political and cultural aspects of the hippie movement. Some names to include are Thomas Wolfe, Ken Kesey, Tom Hayden, Abbie Hoffman, The Grateful Dead, Janis Joplin, etc. Find out what they contributed to the 1960s and what they have done since then.

La Causa

Cesar Chavez knew all too well what life was like for migrant workers, many of whom were Mexican Americans. They lived in tents, often did not have a bathroom to use, and traveled from bean fields to walnut groves with the changing crop seasons. The Chavez family became migrant workers when financial problems forced them to give up their farm near Yuma, Arizona, where Cesar Chavez was born in 1927. Young Chavez frequently went hungry and had very little clothing. By the time of his eighth grade graduation, he had attended 38 different schools. With his background experiences, Chavez was the right candidate for a job with the Community Service Organization. This agency helped poor people deal with a variety of problems, including housing, medical care, and legal aid. Chavez wanted to go beyond these basic services, however. He knew that workers were being taken advantage of by the growers. Pay was far below minimum wage, conditions were unsafe, and children were forced to work long hours.

Cesar Chavez

Chavez believed that a union would help the migrant workers obtain fair wages and safe work and living conditions. In 1962 he started talking to farmers, going from farm to farm, and organized the National Farm Workers Association. The labor union staged a strike against grape growers in 1965. More attention was needed for *La Causa* to be successful, so Chavez organized a 300-mile march across California. At Chavez's urging, some university students and religious leaders joined the farm workers to help them publicize the cause. When many growers still refused to sign contracts with the union, Chavez called for a boycott. He asked the American people not to buy grapes grown in California. The tactic finally worked. Chavez's union eventually became a part of the United Farm Workers Organizing Committee. In 1970 the name was changed to United Farm Workers of America, but its purpose remained the same. Chavez continued to lead the cause of improving working conditions for farm workers until his death in 1993.

Suggested Activities

Walk in His Shoes Go on a one-mile walk. Record the time. Figure out how long it would take to walk 300 miles. Speculate what such a long walk would be like.

Discussion Discuss either of these topics: the effectiveness of labor unions or the effectiveness of boycotts and strikes.

Conscience Cesar Chavez followed his conscience when he led strikes and boycotts against the growers. Some Americans were sympathetic to his cause while others sided with the growers. Whose side do you agree with and why?

More Learn more about Cesar Chavez and his cause. See Teacher Created Materials book *#605 Interdisciplinary Unit—Heroes*.

"Conscience of the Court"

African American Thurgood Marshall was born in Baltimore in 1908. When young Marshall got into trouble at school, the principal assigned sections from the United States Constitution for the boy to memorize. Later this information proved invaluable to him when he argued court cases.

Marshall went on to graduate with honors from Lincoln University in Pennsylvania. After finishing first in his class at Howard University Law School in Washington, D.C., he entered private practice. His specialty was civil rights cases.

Marshall moved to New York City in 1938 when he became the special counsel for the NAACP. During his years with the organization, he rose to the position of director and counselor of the Legal Defense and Education Fund. In 1939 Marshall was admitted to practice in the Supreme Court. Throughout his career, he won 29 of the 32 cases he argued there. Perhaps the best known case Marshall argued was *Brown v.*

Thurgood Marshall

The Board of Education of Topeka, Kansas, in which he challenged school segregation. During this famous 1954 case, he said that segregated education could not result in equal education and that it placed black children at a disadvantage. Even though the Court agreed and the states were ordered to integrate their schools, the ruling was met with resistance. One district in Virginia closed its schools for five years rather than comply with the Supreme Court ruling.

Marshall was appointed to the bench as a judge in the Second Circuit Court of Appeals. In 1965 President Johnson appointed him solicitor general of the Department of Justice. Two years later Johnson appointed Marshall to serve as a justice on the United States Supreme Court. As the first African American to hold this office, Marshall continued to work for equal justice for all until his resignation on June 27, 1991. Thurgood Marshall died in 1993, but his legacy lives on in the lasting contributions he made to the American justice system.

Suggested Activities

Quote Thurgood Marshall said, "Like an eating cancer, segregation destroys the morale of our citizens and disfigures our country throughout the world." Respond in writing to this statement.

Discussion The *Brown v. The Board of Education* case became one of the most important cases ever brought before the Supreme Court. Discuss how it indirectly affected almost every school in the United States.

Memorize Marshall had to memorize sections of the United States Constitution. Memorize the Preamble. Take turns reciting it aloud.

40

An Entertainment Overview

From a newspaper, television programming guide, and other resources find a list of the top 10 shows on TV and the top 10 movies at the box office. Ask the students to briefly identify the concept of each. Compare them to the following popular sixties programs and movies.

On TV

The Dick Van Dyke Show This groundbreaking show ruled the sixties and made Mary Tyler Moore America's sweetheart.

Wide World of Sports Premiering in 1961, this show featured popular as well as little-known sports such as gymnastics and ski jumping.

I Spy This show about secret agents was the first to pair a black actor and a white actor as protagonists. Bill Cosby and Robert Culp starred in the dramatic series.

Star Trek This science-fiction series was cancelled only three seasons after its debut in 1966. It remained hugely popular in reruns well into the nineties and spawned several movies and other TV series.

Rowan and Martin's Laugh-In On January 22, 1968, this show premiered on the NBC TV network. Its controversial and biting political humor made it an overnight sensation.

Julia In 1968 Diahann Carroll became the first African American female to star in her own TV show.

The Smothers Brothers Comedy Hour A hit with viewers, the variety show was cancelled by the network in 1969 due to its outspoken, liberal, antiwar views.

Sesame Street In November 1969 Jim Henson and his Muppets first made their appearance on this special show for young children. A milestone in educational TV, it employed new techniques for teaching children the alphabet as well as math.

At the Movies

Dr. No This 1962 film was the first of the hugely profitable James Bond films.

Cleopatra At 43 million dollars, this was the most expensive film to date. Richard Burton and Elizabeth Taylor starred.

Beach Blanket Bingo Part of a series starring Annette Funicello and Frankie Avalon, these cheaply made films were aimed at the teenage audience.

Bonnie and Clyde After the release of this film, gangster fashions were all the rage. It depicted violence and bloodshed more graphically than earlier films.

The Sound of Music The 1965 Academy Award Best Picture remains a family classic.

The Graduate Dustin Hoffman and Anne Bancroft starred in this 1967 story of a college graduate who questions the values and lifestyle of his parents.

2001: A Space Odyssey This 1968 Oscar-winning film set a new standard for visual effects in movies.

Easy Rider Jack Nicholson, Peter Fonda, and Dennis Hopper starred in this 1969 hit about two hippie motorcyclists who ride across the U.S.A. and pick up a small-town lawyer along the way.

Suggested Activities

Poll Conduct a poll and find out with which television programs and movies your class is familiar.

James Bond Find out how many different actors have played the role of James Bond. List the names of the actors and the titles of the films.

Cleopatra At the time, *Cleopatra* was the most expensive film ever made. What film currently holds this record?

Sidney Poitier

Sidney Poitier is one of the most important African American figures ever to have worked in Hollywood. His groundbreaking roles paved the way for today's group of popular black actors.

Poitier was born in 1924 to a Bahamian couple in Miami, Florida. Most of his childhood was spent in the West Indies, but when he was 16 years old, he returned to Miami. From there he traveled to New York City and worked at a number of odd jobs, including dishwashing. When an ad in the newspaper called for actors at the American Negro Theatre in Harlem, Poitier applied for a role. After his somewhat wooden audition he was admonished by the director that he was no actor and could not be one. Undeterred, he spent six months training to overcome his strong West Indian accent. He also spent four years in the U.S. Army and on his return tried out again at the American Negro Theatre. This time he was accepted and was able to join an elite group of

Sidney Poitier

African American actors that included Harry Belafonte, Ossie Davis, and Ruby Dee. In 1946 Poitier landed a small role in an all-black Broadway production of *Lysistrata*. He was so nervous that he fumbled some of his lines, and the audience laughed. Critics praised his comic abilities. Poitier continued to work in other American Negro Theatre productions, the most important of which was *A Raisin in the Sun.*

Throughout the fifties Poitier starred in a number of dramatic films including *Blackboard Jungle* and *Cry*. It was the 1958 movie *The Defiant Ones* that made him a star. Poitier's next major role was in the film version of the Broadway hit *A Raisin in the Sun*. Although many critics felt his performance deserved an Oscar nomination, it was his role in the 1963 film *Lilies of the Field* that won him the coveted Best Actor award. In doing so, he became the first African American to win an Academy Award for Best Actor. Later sixties films saw him as a teacher of a group of poor white students in *To Sir With Love; Guess Who's Coming to Dinner* cast him as the fiance of a wealthy white woman.

During the seventies, Poitier switched from acting to directing. With films such as *Stir Crazy*, he featured a new generation of black actors, including Denise Nicholas and Richard Pryor. Humor was featured in these films while politics took a back seat.

Although not as active in the industry as he once was, Sidney Poitier continues to bring a dignity and compassion to his roles. As one of the first African American actors to portray a hero in a leading part, he left an indelible mark on Hollywood.

Suggested Activities

Since Then Find out if any black actors have won Academy Awards since Poitier.

Research What is the play *Lysistrata* about? Explain it in your own words.

A Hollywood Legend

She was named for two screen legends—Norma Talmadge and Jean Harlow. Norma Jean Baker only lived to be 36 years old, yet she left a lasting impression on popular fashion for years to come. As Marilyn Monroe, this actress became a true Hollywood legend.

Norma Jean was born June 1, 1926. Her mother, Gladys Baker Mortenson, was a 24-year-old divorcee. Her biological father was C. Stanley Gifford, a salesman who worked with Gladys at a Hollywood film lab. Gifford refused to marry Mortenson and was never seen by her or his daughter again. While Gladys Mortenson spent time in and out of hospitals for treatment of mental illness, her daughter lived in twelve different foster homes and in an orphanage for awhile. Many of her days were spent in movie theaters where she dreamed of becoming a movie star. When she was just 16, young Mortenson married 21-year-old merchant marine James Dougherty.

Marilyn Monroe

Discovered by a photographer when she worked in a weapons plant, she became a model. After divorcing her husband, she took her mother's family name and was known as Norma Jean Baker. Her modeling drew the attention of a film studio. Renamed Marilyn Monroe, she had a few small film roles in the late 1940s. It was the 1952 film *Gentlemen Prefer Blondes* that propelled her to stardom. The next year, she married baseball great Joe DiMaggio, but the union did not last. One year later they were divorced. Weary of the constant pressure of being in the public eye, Monroe began taking sleeping pills at night and often drank alcohol to stay relaxed. By 1955 Monroe was ready for more serious roles. She had grown tired of playing the beautiful dumb blonde. At the Actors Studio in New York she studied acting with the great master, Lee Strasberg. When Monroe returned to Hollywood, she formed her own production company and starred in the hits *Bus Stop* and *The Seven Year Itch*. In 1956 she married American playwright Arthur Miller, but they divorced a few years later. Several more successful films followed. Her last movie, in 1961, *The Misfits*, was especially written for her by her ex-husband Arthur Miller. The following year Marilyn Monroe was found dead in her home, a victim of an overdose of sleeping pills.

Since her death, she has become a pop icon and is immortalized as one of the great movie legends of all time.

Suggested Activities

Warhol Marilyn Monroe was the subject of one of Andy Warhol's famous paintings. Display a copy of this print and write an appropriate title for it.

Modern Monroe Eighties and nineties music pop star Madonna is often compared to Marilyn Monroe. Make a Venn diagram of the two entertainers' likenesses and differences.

The Sports Scene

As sports enjoyed wider TV coverage throughout the sixties, they attracted more money and became more businesslike. It was during this decade that manufacturers began advertising their brand names on racing cars, for example. Read about some important events in the sixties world of sports.

- *Wide World of Sports* premiered on TV on April 29, 1961. Shown on Saturday afternoons, the program popularized little-known sports such as wrestling and gymnastics.

- Bowling was a national craze, and bowling alleys provided a new nighttime hangout for teenagers.

- Surfing was popular on the beaches of California and Hawaii. Surf fashions, surf music, and another sport, skateboarding, grew out of the surf culture. Popular surf music groups included the Beach Boys, the Ventures, and Jan and Dean.

- Golfing remained a favorite recreation, even among the presidents. On the pro circuit during the sixties Arnold Palmer remained dominant, winning the Masters title three times as well as the British and the U.S. Open.

- Women's tennis came a long way with the help of Billie Jean King. King learned to play on public courts and fought her way to the top of the tennis world, winning three Wimbledon titles in succession from 1966 to 1968. She championed equality for women in sports and professionalism in tennis. Previously there was no money in tennis, but King lobbied for competition for cash prizes. The next hurdle involved equitable pay for men and women players. Prizes for men's tournaments were much higher than for women's. In protest, Billie Jean and eight other top women players quit the USLTA (United States Lawn Tennis Association) to form their own tour. It was a success, and today's players continue to benefit from King's work.

- Boxing had its own hero in Cassius Clay. After joining the Black Muslims, he changed his name to Muhammed Ali. When called by the draft in 1967, he refused to do military service and was stripped of the heavyweight championship which he had held for three years. The former 1960 Olympic gold medalist became a hero to young African American radicals for his actions.

- The 1968 Olympic Games in Mexico City proved to be controversial when two United States medalists raised fists in recognition of the black movement. Tommy Smith and John Carlos displayed the salute while the American national anthem was being played. They were both suspended from the games.

Suggested Activities

Sports Status Which sixties sports are still popular? Name new sports that have been introduced in the past 10 years.

Heroes Brainstorm a list of some current famous sports figures. Explain how they differ from sixties athletes.

Fastest Woman in the World

Wilma Rudolph

Wilma Rudolph was a born fighter. The seventeenth of nineteen children, she contracted double pneumonia and scarlet fever early in her life. Fortunately, she survived both. Some years later a bout with polio left one of her legs crippled. Rudolph's determined mother took her to doctors in Nashville, and they provided her with unique water and heat therapy. For many years Rudolph had to wear a leg brace, but with the help and encouragement of her large family, she was able to run and play without a brace before she entered her teen years.

In junior high school she joined a basketball team and also began running track. Her many wins at track meets did not go unnoticed. Ed Temple, a coach from Tennessee State College, was particularly impressed when he watched her compete in 1956. The coach invited Rudolph to compete in a summer college athletic program. She went to Nashville to train, and on the day of the national track meet was victorious in all nine races that she had entered. Coach Temple continued to train Rudolph, but this time it was for the Olympics. As a member of the 1956 U.S. Women's Olympic Relay Team, she won a bronze medal. For four years she continued her training with Coach Temple at Tennessee State University after winning an athletic scholarship. Italy was the site of the 1960 Olympics. Rudolph entered three races and after winning them all became the first American woman to win three medals in track. Her accomplishments won her the Associated Press title Athlete of the Year. She was also known as the "fastest woman in the world."

After that, Rudolph worked hard to promote interest in sports among young women. She founded the Wilma Rudolph Foundation to help underprivileged children and served as a consultant on minority affairs at DePauw University in Indiana. Wilma Rudolph died in 1994 at the age of 54.

Suggested Activities

Record Holders Rudolph was proclaimed the fastest woman in the world. Find out who currently holds that title. Compare the speed record set by Rudolph with the current recordholder's speed.

Races Run 100-meter and 200-meter races. Make a class graph of your times.

Discussion Discuss the traits that helped Rudolph overcome severe adversities and accomplish what no other American female athlete had been able to do before.

Olympics Find out what other track and field events are conducted in the course of the Olympics. An excellent resource for exploring the topic of the Olympics is Teacher Created Materials #064, *Share the Olympic Dream.*

Prince of the Pittsburgh Pirates

In 1961 he was the batting champion of the year. Five years later he was voted Most Valuable Player of the National League. On July 27, 1970, he became only the eleventh player in the history of baseball to achieve 3,000 hits. Who was this baseball superstar? His name was Roberto Clemente, one of the most popular and well-liked players of his time.

Roberto Clemente

Born in San Juan, Puerto Rico, on August 18, 1934, Clemente's family instilled him with solid values. He was taught to share with others, to be honest, and to work hard for what he needed. When the family could not afford to buy real baseballs for Clemente, he and his friends made their own by wrapping string around old golf balls. He could not wait to enter high school because they had real baseball equipment. Small and shy, Clemente emerged as the best athlete ever to graduate from Vizarrondo High School. He was Most Valuable Player on the track team and made the school's baseball all-star team three years in a row.

After high school he joined a winter baseball team in Puerto Rico. Scouts from the major leagues saw him play, and in 1954 Clemente signed a contract with the Pittsburgh Pirates. A quiet, sensitive man, he always gave 100% to his team, even when he was hurting from recurring muscle problems. His lifetime batting average was .317, and he played on 12 National League All-Star teams during his 18-year career. Numerous honors came his way, and the people of Puerto Rico considered him to be a living symbol of the country.

Although baseball was his first love, Clemente found time to help others in need. He took time to visit sick children and donated money to help others. Late in 1972, he organized a relief committee to aid earthquake victims in Managua, Nicaragua. On New Year's Eve, a plane was loaded with supplies; Clemente was also on board. Moments after takeoff from San Juan Airport, there were explosions and the airplane crashed into the ocean. Clemente's body was never recovered.

In 1973 in a special election, Clemente was elected to the National Baseball Hall of Fame. It was a fitting honor for a man who was a role model both on and off the baseball field.

Suggested Activities

World Series In 1960 and in 1971 Roberto Clemente helped the Pirates to World Series victories. Find out who the Pirates played in each series. List some of Clemente's achievements during those games.

Records Before his death in 1972, Clemente learned that he was the eleventh man in major league history to get 3,000 hits. Research and find the names of any other players who have achieved or surpassed that record.

Nickname Discuss why Roberto Clemente's nickname, Prince of the Pittsburgh Pirates, is an appropriate title.

No Silent Springs

Imagine a silent spring with no chirping birds, bustling insects, or the sounds of nature emerging from the long winter sleep. This chilling scenario is what environmentalist Rachel Carson warned against in her book *Silent Spring*. After a friend alerted Carson, she investigated the aftermath of a bird sanctuary that had been sprayed with the pesticide DDT. Besides killing pesky mosquitoes, it also killed many birds and harmless insects. Carson's concerns about what DDT was doing to the environment went unheeded until her book was published in 1962.

Born in 1907 in Pennsylvania, Rachel Carson enjoyed the nature of both the nearby woods and the ocean, a passion she shared with her mother. An avid reader, Carson planned to become a writer, but a college biology class helped her decide to combine the two careers. They were both put to good use in her job at the U.S. Fish and Wildlife Service. In addition to editing all of their publications, Carson wrote articles on the side. After reading one of Carson's articles, an editor at a publishing firm encouraged her to write a book. In 1948 Carson wrote her first bestseller, *The Sea Around Us*. It stayed at the top of the bestseller list for more than a year. After being awarded a fellowship, Carson was financially able to resign from the Fish and Wildlife Service and devote her time to writing. She purchased a summer home on the coast of Maine and studied the ecology of tide pools. The resulting book, *The Edge of the Sea*, examined the interdependence of all living creatures in seaside communities. It was her publication of *Silent Spring*, though, that gathered the most controversy. While some tried to discredit her work, Carson's message came through loudly and clearly. Eventually, the United States banned the use of DDT. Sadly, Rachel Carson died in 1964 before the impact of her environmental work had been fully realized.

Suggested Activities

Environmentalists Research some other famous environmentalists and learn what they have done to protect the environment.

Oceanographer Sylvia Earle is an oceanographer who is an outspoken protector of marine life. Compare her causes with those of fellow oceanographer Yves Jacques Cousteau.

DDT Find answers to these two questions: What do the letters DDT stand for? What are some other commonly used pecticides and how do they work?

Read Aloud Read some excerpts from *The Sea Around Us* or *Silent Spring*. Discuss the passages.

One Small Step

When President Kennedy was sworn into office in 1961, he vowed to put a man on the moon before the decade was out. Although he did not live long enough to see his dream realized, the nation did witness man's historic voyage to the moon. One of the three astronauts on this momentous mission was Neil Armstrong.

Neil Armstrong

Neil Alden Armstrong was born in 1930 in Wapakoneta, Ohio. During the Korean War he served as a pilot for the U.S. Navy. In 1955 Armstrong graduated from Purdue University and went on to become a civilian test pilot for NASA. At Edwards Air Force Base in Lancaster, California, Armstrong tested the X-15 rocket airplane. When he began astronaut training in 1962, he became the first civilian to join the program. The 1966 *Gemini 8* mission was Armstrong's first flight in space. During this flight, he and his partner, David R. Scott, docked their spacecraft with an unmanned spacecraft. After their spacecraft went into a violent roll, the astronauts were able to get the situation under control and safely return to Earth. Three years later, in 1969, Armstrong was chosen to be the commander of the *Apollo 11* mission to the moon. Fellow astronaut Edwin E. Aldrin (Buzz) landed and walked on the moon with Armstrong while Michael Collins orbited the moon in the command module.

As Armstrong made history by becoming the first person to walk on the moon, the world stopped to watch the event on television. On July 20, 1969, Neil Armstrong stepped onto the moon's rocky surface and uttered these famous words, "That's one small step for (a) man, one giant leap for mankind."

After retiring from NASA in 1971, Neil Armstrong became a professor of aerospace engineering at the University of Cincinnati.

Suggested Activities

Exploration Explore the *Apollo 11* mission further with the reading and activities on page 49.

Moon Map In pairs, draw and label maps of the moon. Include the following landmarks: Sea of Cold, Sea of Rains, Sea of Crises, Sea of Clouds, Sea of Moisture, Sea of Nectar, Sea of Tranquility, and the site of the *Apollo 11* landing. A great resource for this activity is *One Giant Leap* by Mary Ann Fraser (Henry Holt and Company, 1993).

Debate Debate the issue of space exploration. Answer this question and provide defenses for your views: Should the U.S. continue to expand its space program, or should it be reduced?

Mission to the Moon

Make a copy of this page for each small group of students. Direct them to read the paragraphs and complete the critical thinking activities that follow the story.

On the morning of July 16, 1969, three astronauts squeezed through the hatch of the spacecraft that was to be their home for the next eight days. As their families anxiously watched on the ground, Neil Armstrong, Buzz Aldrin, and Michael Collins listened to a voice at launch control count off the last ten seconds. Clouds of steam and smoke billowed around the rocket as all engines ignited and lift off was achieved. Only two and a half minutes into the flight, the *Saturn V's* first stage had shut down and fallen into the ocean. Four seconds later, the second stage separated from the *Columbia*, and the astronauts began to experience weightlessness. After the third and final stage fired, the spacecraft orbited around Earth one and a half times before the spacecraft propelled *Apollo 11* toward the moon. A little over four hours into the flight, the astronauts worked to maneuver the *Eagle* into position. Now they were ready for the job that lay ahead.

On the fifth morning of the mission, the astronauts were awakened by Mission Control. It was landing day, the day for which they had trained. Aldrin and Armstrong moved into *Eagle* while Collins stayed behind in *Columbia*. When Collins released the hatch, the two modules drifted apart. Less than two hours later, *Eagle* began its descent. Skillfully and carefully the two men piloted the craft toward the Sea of Tranquility. Collins, meanwhile, continued to orbit the back side of the moon. As Neil Armstrong stepped cautiously off the ladder onto the moon's surface, the world watched intently and listened to his words: "That's one small step for (a) man, one giant leap for mankind." A dream had become a reality.

Suggested Activity

Knowledge When was the *Apollo 11* space mission launched? _____

List five facts from the story. Name the three astronauts on the mission. _____

_____

_____

Comprehension Summarize the *Apollo 11* mission in your own words. _____

_____

_____

Application Write about some sights the astronauts would have seen if they had landed on Mars instead of the moon. _____

_____

Analysis Make a list of five things you can conclude about the *Apollo 11* mission. _____

_____

Synthesis On a separate piece of paper, rewrite the story from Michael Collins' point of view.

Evaluation Defend the value of future space exploration. _____

_____

Modern Cooking

Walk into any convenience store and you are likely to find shelves of prepackaged foods ready for eating. All you have to do is heat up the items in the microwave, and in a matter of seconds the food is piping hot.

It is hard to imagine now, but it was not so long ago that microwave ovens were first introduced into American homes. In 1942 Percy LeBaron of the Raytheon Company in Waltham, Massachusetts, accidentally discovered that microwaves used for signal transmissions would cook food. A chocolate bar in his pocket had melted when it came in contact with the signals.

In 1967 the first compact microwave oven for home use was introduced to the United States by Amana, a subsidiary of Raytheon. Read how the microwave oven works. Label the components with the corresponding number.

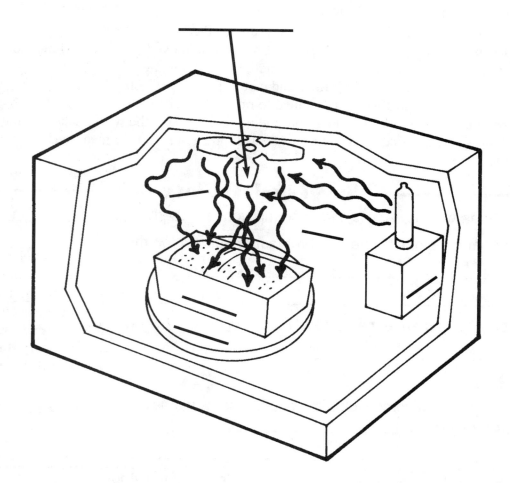

A magnetron (1) produces a beam (2) of microwaves. This microwave beam, which has a high heating power, strikes a spinning fan (3). In turn, the fan reflects the waves onto the food (4) from all directions (5). A turntable (6) moves the food to promote even heating.

Where Are the Wild Things?

All areas of life from politics to fashions were changing radically during the sixties, and the children's book market was no exception. One of the most enduring and often read children's authors and illustrators emerged during this period. His name is Maurice Sendak.

Born on June 10, 1928, Sendak was the youngest of three children born to Philip and Sarah (Schindler) Sendak. As a child, he was sickly after having contracted measles followed by bilateral pneumonia. His reputation as frail made it difficult for him to make friends, and he found that he was not particularly good at sports, not even skating or stoopball. Instead, he stayed home and drew pictures. His peers considered him a sissy. School was no better. Sendak claims he hated it from the first grade on because it stifled his creativity and imagination. However, he did manage to graduate from high school and even attended the Art Students' League for two years.

Maurice Sendak

A number of jobs led to Sendak's future career as a children's book author and illustrator. During high school he worked part time for a comic book syndicate, adapting the newspaper comic strip "Mutt and Jeff" for comic books. One year he and his brother tried to sell their animated wooden toys to F.A.O. Schwartz, the renowned toy store in New York City. Although the store chose not to purchase the toys, they did hire Sendak as a display artist. By 1956 he had written his first book, *Kenny's Window*. It was not his favorite book, but it showed signs of what was to come. After years of writing and illustrating (often illustrating for other authors), Sendak produced one of the most popular yet controversial children's books ever written. The title was *Where the Wild Things Are,* and it features a little boy named Max and a host of unusual looking monsters. Many librarians felt it was too scary for children, but despite this sentiment it was an unprecedented success. In 1964 Sendak was awarded the Caldecott Medal for this book.

Over the years, Maurice Sendak has been the recipient of numerous honors, including the 1970 Hans Christian Andersen Medal for his entire body of work.

Suggested Activities

Reputation Not until he worked with author Ruth Krauss on *A Hole Is to Dig* was Sendak's reputation as an illustrator established. Compare the drawings in Krauss's book with those of *Where the Wild Things Are.*

Controversy Do you think the pictures in *Where the Wild Things Are* are too scary for little children? Draw a page for a new version of the book in which the monsters are tame looking.

Princess of Black Poetry

Her given name is Yolanda Cornelia Giovanni, Jr., but the world knows her better as Nikki Giovanni. This African American poet has been labeled the "Princess of Black Poetry" by some critics for her well-attended poetry readings. Recognition for her work first came in the 1960s. Since then she has been the recipient of a number of awards, including a citation for *Ladies Home Journal* Woman of the Year in 1972.

Nikki Giovanni

Born on June 7, 1943, in Knoxville, Tennessee, Giovanni grew up in a close-knit family. Her father, Jones, was a probation officer and her mother, Yolanda, was a teacher. When she was very young, the family moved to Ohio, but she maintained a special bond with her grandmother, Louvenia, back in Tennessee. In 1960 Giovanni entered Fisk University in Tennessee. At that time her politics were very conservative. Frequent clashes with the dean of women, though, led to her expulsion. A few years later she returned to Fisk, this time as a serious student and black rights activist. After graduating with honors, she did graduate work at the University of Pennsylvania and Columbia University in New York City.

Giovanni turned out to be a prolific writer. Between 1968 and 1970 she published three books of poetry. These writings reflected her life experiences during the sixties and depicted her growth as a black woman. Enormously popular, her book *Black Judgement* sold 6,000 copies in three months, more than five times the number of copies sold by the average book of poetry. In 1969 Giovanni began teaching at Rutgers University in New Jersey and also gave birth to her child, Thomas. During the seventies she wrote two books of poetry for children, *Spin a Soft Black Song* and *Ego Tripping and Other Poems for Young Children.* The poems in these collections revolve around the theme of family while voicing racial pride. She also recorded some of her work, bringing her more fame and recognition. These days Nikki Giovanni lectures and tours throughout the United States and Europe and continues to be a major force in black consciousness.

Suggested Activities

Define Define "ego tripping." Read aloud some poems from her book of the same name. Write your own poems which would be appropriate for that book.

Poetry Reading Take turns reading a Nikki Giovanni poem of your choice to the rest of the class.

The Peanuts Gang

Almost everyone is familiar with that lovable cartoon character, Snoopy, but not everyone may know the creator of this amusing comic strip. His name is Charles M. Schulz, and he was born on November 26, 1922, in Minneapolis, Minnesota. After attending public high school in St. Paul, Minnesota, Schulz submitted cartoons to most of the major magazines. All he received in turn were rejections and no encouragement. From 1943 to 1945 he served with the Twentieth Armored Division in Europe and achieved the rank of staff sergeant. After World War II, he set about in earnest to find work as an artist. An art correspondence school did hire him to correct basic lessons. Several of his coworkers' names there were used in some of his comic strips. During this job, Schulz continued to mail his own cartoons to major syndicates. One editorial director was very interested in his work and invited him to the New York office. After looking at the samples Schulz had brought along, the company decided to publish his *Peanuts* cartoon strip.

Charles M. Schulz

Schulz's numerous awards include the School Bell award from the National Education Association. A Peabody and an Emmy award went to his 1966 CBS cartoon special, *A Charlie Brown Christmas*. Other teleplays followed with Charlie Brown celebrating various holidays. Titles include *It's the Great Pumpkin, Charlie Brown* and *It's the Easter Beagle, Charlie Brown*.

In addition to creating the *Peanuts* comic strip, writing books, and producing teleplays, Schulz did some illustration work for other authors, including Art Linkletter's *Kids Say the Darnedest Things*. With Charlie Brown's introduction to television in 1965, Peanuts subsidiaries manufactured everything from clothing and toys to lunch boxes and stationery. In 1969 Snoopy made international news when his name became the official name of the Lunar Excursion Module of the *Apollo 10* manned flight to the moon.

Peanuts and the gang still enjoy popularity and can be read daily in newspapers across the country.

Suggested Activities

Teleplay Write a new play for Charlie Brown and the gang.

Characters Conduct a class poll to find out which characters are the top three favorites. Alternatively, rank the characters from best liked to least liked.

Cartooning Cut out some *Peanuts* cartoon strips and glue them to a sheet of paper. Block out the dialog in each cartoon strip. Write a dialog for each strip. Students share your cartoons with partners.

15 Minutes of Fame

The sixties was a period of rebellion and radical change on all fronts, including politics, race, women's rights, and even art and culture. One painter in particular captivated and dominated the art scene with his unique way of looking at the world. The artist was Andy Warhol.

Along with fellow painters Claes Oldenburg and James Rosenquist, Warhol had a background in commercial art. Images in his work were based on neon signs, the mass media, and advertising symbols. Coca Cola bottles, Campbell's soup cans, and Brillo boxes became subjects for his work. This type of art became known as "pop art."

Pop art is characterized by shiny colors and snappy designs which are often blown up to gigantic proportions. Overnight, pop became a marketing phenomenon, as well as an art movement. Its instant success was due in part to the fact that it made people look at the world in a different and pleasing way. Warhol wanted people to re-examine their surroundings, and so he made art out of daily life.

Andy Warhol

Born in 1930, Warhol lived with his mother and 25 cats in New York City. He began his career as a shoe illustrator for print ads. In 1960 his acrylic paintings of comic book characters Superman, Batman, and Dick Tracy brought him some recognition. But it was through the soup cans and celebrity posters that he found the most fame. Warhol also made more than 60 films between 1963 and 1968. For the most part, they were about mundane subjects. His silent film *Sleep*, for example, captured six hours of a man sleeping. Although Warhol claimed he wanted anonymity, he was always the center of media attention, and he clamored for the spotlight. With his platinum wig, pale makeup, and dark glasses, he became the symbol for pop art in American culture.

Suggested Activities

Quote Andy Warhol once said, "In the future everyone will be famous for 15 minutes." Explain what he meant by that statement. Have you had your 15 minutes of fame? How?

Soup Cans Display a picture of Warhol's *100 Cans of Campbell's Soup*. A copy can be found in *The Annotated Mona Lisa: A Crash Course in Art History from Prehistoric to Post-Modern* by Carol Strickland, Ph.D. (Andrews and McMeel, 1992). Create your own pop art project. After your class determines a subject, each student can draw a picture of it. Everyone should use the same sized sheet of drawing paper. With clear tape, assemble the completed drawings into a giant art quilt.

Sixties Art

American art took on new dimensions in the sixties. Pop art used images from mass culture in a modified form. Two other movements—op art and minimalism—were also part of the art scene. Explore these art forms with the following projects.

Optical art

Optical art, more commonly known as op art, was developed in the mid-60s by a group of English painters. The style combined color and abstract patterns to create optical illusions and movement. Let students make their own op art pattern with this project.

Materials: white butcher paper, tempera paints (variety of colors), paintbrushes, combs, paper clips, plastic forks and knives, and/or barrettes

Directions: Cover the whole surface of the butcher paper with any color tempera paint (dark colors work best). Run the comb in one direction over the wet paint. Experiment with other materials (paper clips, plastic knives, etc.) to make lines across the paper. Allow to dry before displaying.

Minimalism

Minimalism is a form of minimum art. The look is clean, bare, and simple. In the sixties it replaced the vulgarity and vibrance of pop art with cold, mechanical forms. Panes of glass on a gallery floor and metal shelves attached to a wall constituted one artist's

work. Have students create their own minimal art with the following project.

Materials: variety of cardboard boxes (cube tissue boxes work well); black, white, or blue construction paper; clear tape; scissors

Directions: Pair or group the students and direct them to construct a minimalist project out of boxes. Instruct the pairs to cover all their boxes with the same color construction paper, taping the paper to the boxes. Arrange the boxes into a pleasing structure. Let the pairs name their projects; display all completed works. Pop art was not limited to Warhol (see page 54). American Roy Lichtenstein enlarged comic strip panels to billboard size and used bright primary colors with black and white to parody the mindless violence of comic strips. Students can make their own enlarged comic strip art with this project.

Materials: black and white comic strips, access to a photocopy machine, colored marking pens

Directions: Choose one panel from a comic strip (look for one that shows a lot of action). Enlarge the panel on the copy machine. Use bright markers to add color.

Music That Changed the World

After World War II (1939–45) millions of ex-servicemen and their wives had families. By the 1960s these "baby boomers" were teenagers. Rebelling against their conservative parents, they began wearing innovative clothes, experimented with drugs, and listened to music which reflected their rebellious spirit. Some of the major music trends are outlined below.

Pop When Chubby Checker released "Let's Twist Again," the dance became an international fad. It also started a revolution in the way people danced. Partners faced one another but did not touch. The Jerk, the Mashed Potato, and the Locomotion soon followed.

Surf Music In the early sixties surfing became popular on beaches in California and Hawaii. The sport created a nationwide craze and even spawned its own look and way of talking. Several groups created music which evoked the carefree California 60s, but none was more successful than the Beach Boys. From "Surfin' U.S.A." to "Little Deuce Coupe," the emphasis was on fun.

Protest Singers Young folk singers began writing songs about war and social injustice. Popular titles included "We Shall Overcome" and "Blowin' in the Wind." Joan Baez, Bob Dylan, and Phil Ochs were prominent protest singers of the time.

British Invasion When the Beatles invaded the United States, their new sounds and look took the nation by storm (see page 57), eclipsing American groups who had set the style in pop music. Other British bands followed, including the Who, the Animals, the Kinks, and the ever-enduring Rolling Stones.

Psychedelia Some adventurous groups began to experiment with different sounds for their music, and the result was psychedelia which suggested dreamy, mystical states. The Grateful Dead and Jefferson Airplane wowed audiences in San Francisco with their psychedelic tunes. The Beatles joined the crowd with the release of their album *Sergeant Pepper's Lonely Hearts Club Band*.

Bubblegum In stark contrast to the harsh sounds of rock, "bubblegum" music appeared at the end of the sixties. Record companies aimed their music at younger teenagers. The Archies' "Sugar Sugar" is a classic example of the "bubblegum" sound.

Soul Until the late 1950s black music was not allowed to be played on white radio stations. Aretha Franklin's song "Respect" was a phenomenal success and led the way for soul music's acceptance by white audiences.

Suggested Activities

Varieties What is your favorite type of music? Identify any new categories that did not exist in the sixties.

Perseverance The Beach Boys, the Rolling Stones, the Grateful Dead and other sixties groups enjoyed success some thirty years after they first came onto the music scene. Choose a group and write an update of where they are now.

Beatlemania

Their first hit, "Love Me Do," reached only number seventeen on British music charts in 1962, but their powerful "beat" and distinctive haircuts helped them stand out from other groups. With the release of "She Loves You" in 1963, the Beatles began a string of major hits. After an appearance on American television in 1964, they enjoyed phenomenal success. At one point, they held the top five spots on U.S. charts—a feat that has yet to be repeated. Quite possibly, the Beatles are the most famous musical group in history.

Just how did four boys from Liverpool make it so big? Their story began in 1957 when John Lennon invited 15 year-old Paul McCartney to join his group, the Quarrymen. Guitarist George Harrison and drummer Pete Best had joined the group by August 1961. In 1962 Best was replaced by Ringo Starr. After record store owner Brian Epstein became their manager, they signed with a recording company. It was not long before the Beatles became England's biggest-ever idols. Their live performances were accompanied by unprecedented hordes of screaming fans. After their February 1964 appearance on *The Ed Sullivan Show*, "the Fab Four," as they were sometimes called, became transatlantic chart-toppers. While their first albums had combined pop-soul songs with some of Lennon's and McCartney's original compositions, later albums reflected the whole group's efforts. They even wrote scores for their own films. *Help!* and *A Hard Day's Night* depicted their lives and the hysteria that followed them. In 1966 the Beatles gave up touring to concentrate on studio work. The resulting *Revolver* album has been regarded by many as their finest work, but the most innovative was *Sergeant Pepper's Lonely Hearts Club Band*. Released in 1967, the album was an eclectic mix of styles, combining psychedelia with symphonic sounds. More changes were in the future as the Beatles explored Eastern religion with the Maharishi Mahesh Yogi. After their manager died, they set up their own record company and released "Hey, Jude," their best-selling single. Other albums and a third movie, *Yellow Submarine*, followed, but in 1970 the Beatles broke up their partnership. Ten years later, John Lennon was fatally wounded outside of his New York City apartment building, denying forever a possible, much-rumored reunion.

Suggested Activities

Response "The Beatles were, quite simply, phenomenal. They changed lives, they changed pop music, they changed the world." Write a response to this quote.

Investigate Find out more about the three remaining Beatles, Paul, George, and Ringo. What paths have their careers followed?

Counterculture's Finest Moment

During the 1960s many young people embraced a lifestyle that was totally different from that of their conservative parents. They questioned everything and refused to conform to society's standards. These baby boomers developed a distinctive style of dress (page 60) and music, as well as their own lingo. "Far out!," "Peace, brother," and "What's happenin'?" were three commonly heard phrases. Some adopted a hippie look and lived in communes while others joined radical political groups. Each of these groups had one thing in common: They rejected all symbols of authority, especially their parents and the government. They became known as the "counterculture."

For three days in August 1969, Woodstock in upstate New York became the focus of the counterculture revolution. During the idyllic weekend 400,000 people partied peacefully and were part of one huge, loving community. Organizers Michael Lang and Artie Kornfield had spent six months planning the show at the 600-acre farm. Richie Havens, a little known African American folk singer, opened the proceedings which were stopped twice by rain. Musicians, including Janis Joplin, The Grateful Dead, Jimi Hendrix, Jefferson Airplane, Bob Dylan, Joan Baez, Ravi Shankar, Santana, and Crosby, Stills, Nash and Young, entertained the crowd with their own personal styles. From protest to rock to psychedelic, all kinds of music could be enjoyed there. Santana stole the show with "Soul Sacrifice." Jimi Hendrix closed the adventure with an ear-splitting version of "The Star-Spangled Banner." Despite the lack of sanitation and low food and medical supplies, the concert-goers stayed and rocked on to the largest outdoor, overnight festival ever held. Later that same year, the Rolling Stones, unable to attend Woodstock, gave a free concert at Altamont, California. It turned deadly when a man in the crowd pulled a gun and was knifed to death by a Hell's Angel member. The spell of Woodstock was broken, dealing a serious blow to future outdoor festivals.

Suggested Activities

Drug Scene Drugs were rampant at Woodstock. LSD was used to spike drinks backstage. Audience members smoked pot openly. Find out the short-term and long-term side effects of these drugs. For more information see *Focus on Hallucinogens* by Jeffrey Shulman (Twenty-First Century Books, 1991).

Discuss Do you think there could ever be another Woodstock? Defend your answers.

Reunion Woodstock II was held in 1994 for the twenty-fifth anniversary of the original festival. Research to see who performed, who attended, and how it was similar to or different from the first Woodstock festival.

1960s Inventors and Inventions

A multitude of advances in technology in the 1960s changed the American lifestyle. New devices led to quicker and easier communication, and inexpensive electrical goods became available to ordinary people. Read about some of these devices below. Then read through the activities listed below and choose one to complete.

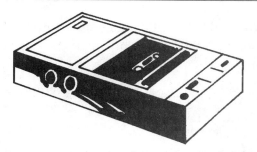

- One of the most important inventions of the era was the computer. At first it was used for data processing and was an extremely bulky machine, sometimes taking up whole rooms.

- In the early 1960s teenagers listened to their favorite tunes on small portable record players with monaural sound. Stereo discs did not become available until the midsixties when powerful hi-fi systems and stereo headphones made their debut.

- Along with stereo systems, cassette tape recorders were first marketed in 1963.

- A number of small electric appliances debuted during the sixties including electric toothbrushes (first manufactured in 1961) and heated hair curlers.

- Fibertip pens were first manufactured in the sixties.

- Improved printing techniques helped posters become a cheap way to decorate a home. Immensely popular, they often depicted images of pop stars and older movie stars.

- In 1962 the first communications satellite, *Telstar,* began relaying pictures across the Atlantic, making it possible to report global news instantaneously.

- The first laser was made during the sixties. An acronym for Light Amplification by Stimulated Emission of Radiation, the laser has an intense beam of pure light which is capable of cutting through metal. In 1963 the first hologram, using lasers, was devised. Today, the laser has been perfected so accurately that it is routinely used for many types of surgeries.

Suggested Activities

Comparisons Compare early stereo equipment with the stereo equipment of today. How do they differ in size and in the quality of sound produced?

Records Teenagers in the sixties listened to their favorite songs on $33\frac{1}{3}$ records and long-playing albums. What did these records look like and are they available today? What has now replaced records?

Posters Posters in the sixties typically bore psychedelic images of pop stars such as Bob Dylan, Jimi Hendrix, and Mick Jagger. Draw psychedelic posters of your favorite pop stars.

Inventors Research and find out about the inventors of any of the advances cited above. For example, Theodore Maiman was the first to develop the laser.

Lasers Although the laser has become an important tool for surgery, it was not originally intended for that use. Do some research to find out some other ways that lasers figure into our daily lives.

Sixties Fashion Trends

Probably the greatest change in fashions came about during the 1960s when new and daring styles were embraced by the youth of America. Read about some of these fashion innovations in the paragraphs below.

Materials Plastics, metals, and even paper were used to create new kinds of clothing. Transparent plastic dresses had to be wiped clean. They would have melted in a hot wash. Disposable paper clothes were meant to be worn only once and then thrown away.

Hemlines Short skirts were not new to the sixties, but the miniskirt was. Introduced in 1965 by English designer Mary Quant, these skirts barely covered the buttocks. Their midthigh lengths made wearing stockings impractical, so Quant introduced tights which were to be worn underneath the minis. Later in the sixties pantyhose were developed and quickly replaced stockings and garter belts.

Boots Leather boots completed the sixties' look. Typically, boots were knee-high with chunky heels.

Pants Two styles of pants dominated the sixties' scene. In the midsixties, hiphuggers were fashionable, but by the end of the decade they had been replaced with bell bottom pants which became wildly popular. Pantsuits for women also became very popular and fashionable.

Makeup The midsixties look consisted of heavy eye makeup, including false eyelashes. Long, straight hair was in. Some women even ironed theirs to straighten it. Teased, bouffant hairdos were also trendy. Later the bob—a short, slanted cut—was introduced by English stylist Vidal Sassoon.

The Unisex Look One of the most enduring trends of the sixties is the unisex look which consisted of denim jeans and a T-shirt. Males and females sported the look.

Twiggy Thin was in, but Twiggy was ultrathin. A famous fashion model, Twiggy was one of London's most famous personalities with her boyish body and large eyes.

Hippies Belief in individual expression led to the hippie look. Favorite styles included caftans, heavy velvet clothes, sheepskin coats, and leather sandals. Beads, vests, and long hair completed the look. Large Afros were worn by some African Americans.

Feelin' Groovy

This crossword puzzle will tell you how well you know your fashions of the sixties. A list of words to choose from can be found at the bottom of this page.

Across

2. a popular hair style worn by Jackie Kennedy
6. disposable clothes were made of this
7. a hat that was part of the Jackie look
9. trousers with a flared leg
12. a cap made popular by folk singers
14. leather, strappy ones were popular with hippies
15. transparent fashions that had to be wiped clean
16. a standard in casual clothes
17. long, flowing robes worn by hippies

Down

1. plastic jewelry with pieces that could be added on
3. frizzed-out hair worn by some African Americans
4. Rudi Gernreich introduced a topless version
5. worn with the miniskirt, especially white ones
8. a style of pants that rode below the waist
10. created by Mary Quant in 1965
11. T-shirts colored for psychedelic effect
13. designed to be worn under the miniskirt

Word List

jeans	hiphuggers	plastic	tights
Dutchboy	caftans	bell bottoms	Afro
bathing suit	miniskirt	poppit beads	
paper	pillbox	boots	
bouffant	sandals	tie-dyed	

Elsewhere . . .

This chronology gives a few of the important events around the globe during the 1960s. Have students research further any people and events that interest them.

1960

- Nikita Khrushchev becomes premier of the USSR.
- Cyprus and the Congo become independent.
- Mrs. Bandaranaike in Sri Lanka becomes the world's first woman prime minister.

1961

- Communists build the Berlin Wall across the city of Berlin to prevent East German citizens from fleeing to West Germany.
- Soviet Cosmonaut Yuri Gagarin becomes the first man in space.

1962

- Uganda and Tanganyika become independent nations.

1963

- On June 11, Buddhist monk Thich Quang Duyc sets himself on fire to protest South Vietnam's President Ngo Dinh Diem.
- South Vietnam's President Ngo Dinh Diem is assassinated.
- Valentina Tereshkova of the Soviet Union becomes the first woman in space.

1964

- Tanzania and Zambia are founded.
- Malta and Malawi become independent.
- Communist leader Nikita Khrushchev is removed from office in the USSR.
- A group of Palestinian Arabs led by Yasser Arafat forms the PLO (Palestinian Liberation Organization) which carries out terrorist attacks.
- China acquires the atomic bomb.

1965

- War breaks out between India and Pakistan.
- Japan's bullet train opens with average speeds of over 100 mph.
- Soviet Cosmonaut Alexei Leonov makes the first space walk.

1966

- Cultural Revolution is launched in China.
- China's Chairman Mao begins a plan to revitalize communism and attacks all capitalist or Western influences.
- The Biafran War rages.
- Guyana becomes independent.
- The Soviet probe *Luna 9* lands on the moon and takes photographs and samples of soil.

1967

- The Six Day War begins when Israeli planes attack air bases in Egypt, Syria, and Jordan.
- The King of Greece is exiled after a coup.
- In India, Indira Gandhi becomes the first woman elected to lead a democracy.

1968

- The Soviet Union and its allies invade Czechoslovakia, forcefully ending the period of openness known as the Prague Spring.
- In Paris, students and workers revolt.
- A massive Tet offensive is mounted in Vietnam.

1969

- Cultural Revolution comes to an end in China.

Images of the Sixties

Use this page to determine what students know about important world events of the 1960s. Make a transparency of this page to be used on an overhead projector. Read a description and call on students to choose the correct answer from the list below. After all the items have been read and discussed, group the students and assign a different topic to each group for further research.

Cultural Revolution	Cuban Missile Crisis
Prague Spring	The Six-Day War
Berlin Wall	Invasion of Czechoslovakia
War in Biafra	Student Revolution

1. Over one million people died in the fighting that broke out after the Eastern region of Nigeria declared its own independence. Thousands of civilians died of starvation and disease during this period from 1966–1970.

2. During June of 1967 the Israelis, believing that another war was about to start, launched an attack on Egypt. Jordan and Syria were drawn into the fighting, and Israel occupied new areas.

3. China's leader, Mao Tse-Tung, broke with the Russians and determined to make China a true Communist state run by its workers. His reforms were so severe that in 1968 the army stepped in to restore order.

4. In 1968 this protest nearly brought down the French government. Unrest began with overcrowding in the educational system. By May of 1968 students occupied the University of Sorbonne in Paris and had set up barricades to ward off the police.

5. When Alexander Dubchek came to power in 1968, his reforms, which gave more freedom to the people, worried Soviet authorities. In August Soviet tanks invaded the country, and Dubchek's government was overthrown.

6. After learning that the Soviets had built missile sites in Cuba, the United States demanded that the missiles be removed from the island. The United States set up a blockade around Cuba, and tensions mounted. Finally, Khrushchev agreed to remove the missiles.

7. In 1961 Soviet leader Nikita Khrushchev demanded that the United States withdraw from West Berlin. When President Kennedy refused to give in, the Soviets built a wall between East and West Berlin.

8. Alexander Dubchek, a liberal, became leader of the Czechoslovakian Communist Party in 1968. He introduced laws to give people greater freedom. This period was later put down by invading Soviet forces.

Answers (*Fold under before copying*): 1. War in Biafra 2. The Six-Day War 3. Cultural Revolution 4. Student Revolution 5. Invasion of Czechoslovakia 6. Cuban Missile Crisis 7. Berlin Wall 8. Prague Spring

To the Bottom of the Sea

A world record was set in January of 1960 when the bathyscaphe *Trieste* descended 35,800 feet (10,912 m) into the Mariana Trench. On board were Auguste Piccard, the French inventor of the *Trieste,* and United States Navy Lieutenant Don Walsh. Learn more interesting facts about this historic voyage by completing the sentences below with antonyms for the words in parentheses.

1. The Mariana Trench, the (shallowest) _____ place on Earth, lies in the Pacific Ocean.

2. Its deepest point is called Challenger Deep and is 36,198 feet (11,033 m) (up) _____ .

3. The Mariana Trench has nearly all the features found on land: plains or flat areas, mountains, and trenches or deep, (wide) _____valleys.

4. Compared to the (lowest) _____ mountain on Earth, Mount Everest in Asia, the deepest point of the Mariana Trench is one mile deeper than the mountain is high.

5. Until the trench was explored, scientists believed that deep areas of the ocean were (lively) _____ .

6. Water pressure on the sea floor is 1,000 times greater than the pressure at the (bottom) _____ of the ocean.

7. It is also very dark and (torrid) _____ there.

8. Animals who live at these depths have adaptations that allow them to (perish) _____ .

9. For example, some deep-sea creatures produce their own (dark) _____ .

10. Anglerfish have lights on their heads while squids have (dim) _____ spots on their arms.

11. Many deep-sea animals are (tiny) _____ and grow to far greater lengths than their cousins in shallower water.

12. A deep-water sea urchin, for example, can grow to a foot (30.48 cm) (narrow) _____.

13. The *Trieste* enabled scientists to find out (few) _____ important facts about (death) _____ in the deepest areas of the ocean.

14. The weight of the *Trieste* enabled it to (sink) _____ .

15. Gasoline tanks, which are (heavier) _____ than the water, float the craft up to the surface.

Suggested Activities

Subs Make your own submarines with an eyedropper, clear plastic bottle, and water. See *Mr. Wizard's Supermarket Science* by Don Herbert (Random House, 1980) for complete directions.

Research Work in small groups to research how a submarine works. Create a flow chart showing the steps involved.

Answers (*Fold under before copying*) 1. deepest 2. down 3. narrow 4. highest 5. lifeless 6. surface 7. cold 8. survive 9. light 10. glowing 11. large 12. wide 13. many, life 14. float 15. lighter (Accept reasonable answers.)

Women of the Olympics

During the 1960, 1964, and 1968 Olympic Games, a number of women distinguished themselves with record-setting performances. See how well you know the female Olympic athletes of the sixties decade. Write the name of the correct athlete on the line at the beginning of each sentence. Use the name box below and reference books to help determine who did what.

1. _____This Australian swimmer won her third straight Olympic gold in the 100-meter swim at the 1964 Tokyo games.

2. _____She won the gold in women's figure skating at the 1968 Winter Olympics in Grenoble.

3. _____She was the first African American woman to win the gold in the 800-meter run.

4. _____In 1960 she became the first African American woman to win three gold medals in track at a single Olympics.

5. _____This speed skater for the Soviet Union won four gold medals in the 1964 Olympic Games at Innsbruck, Austria.

6. _____At the 1964 Tokyo Olympics, this Czechoslovakian won three gold and two silver medals in gymnastics.

7. _____This African American became the first person to win two straight Olympic sprint titles (Tokyo and Mexico City).

8. _____A Soviet gymnast, she introduced ballet into gymnastics and won 18 Olympic medals between 1956 and 1964.

9. _____She performed the first double jump in women's figure skating at the 1960 Squaw Valley, California, games.

10. _____This German won the first gold medal in women's luge at the 1964 Innsbruck Olympics.

11. _____Beginning in 1956, she represented the United States in track and field in five Olympic games and is the only athlete in her sport to do so.

12. _____At the 1968 games in Mexico City, she became the first woman to light the Olympic flame.

Lydia Skoblikova	Vera Caslavska	Larissa Latynina
Carol Heiss	Enriquetta Bassilio	Willye White
Wyomia Tyus	Wilma Rudolph	Madeline Manning
Peggy Fleming	Otrun Enderlein	Dawn Fraser

References

Grace & Glory: A Century of Women in the Olympics by Jane Leder (Triumph Books, 1996)

Olympic Black Women by Martha Ward Plowden (Pelican Publishing Company, 1996)

The Story of the Olympics by Dave Anderson (Beechtree Paperback Book, 1996)

Timetables of Sports History: The Olympic Games by William S. Jarrett (Facts on File, 1990)

Passages

Births

1960
- John Fitzgerald Kennedy, Jr.
- Bono, lead vocalist for U2
- Carol Alt and Kim Alexis, supermodels

1961
- Heather Locklear, actress
- Dennis Rodman, basketball superstar

1962
- Demi Moore and Tom Cruise, actors
- Jackie Joyner Kersee, track star

1963
- Michael Jordan, basketball great
- Whitney Houston, singer/actress

1964
- Melissa Gilbert, actress
- Jose Canseco, baseball star

1965
- Brooke Shields, model/actress

1966
- Mike Tyson, boxing titan
- Janet Jackson, performer

1968
- Molly Ringwald, actress
- Adam Graves, NY Rangers MVP in 1993

Deaths

1960
- Richard Wright, African American novelist

1962
- Marilyn Monroe, actress
- Eleanor Roosevelt, former first lady

1963
- John Fitzgerald Kenndy, U.S. President

1964
- Herbert Hoover, former U.S. President
- General Douglas MacArthur

1965
- Sir Winston Churchill, former leader of England
- Malcolm X, religious leader and political activist

1966
- Walt Disney, filmmaker
- Margaret Sanger, founder of the birth control movement
- Joseph Francis (Buster) Keaton, star of silent films
- Admiral Chester Nimitz, commander of the Pacific fleet in WWII

1967
- Carl Sandburg, Pulitzer Prize winning poet
- Spencer Tracy, Academy Award winning actor
- Henry Luce, founder of *Time, Life* and *Fortune* magazines

1968
- Robert F. Kennedy, former U.S. attorney general and presidential hopeful
- Martin Luther King, Jr., civil rights leader and orator

1969
- Dwight D. Eisenhower, former U.S. president
- Judy Garland, singer and actress
- Joseph P. Kennedy, former chair of SEC and ambassador to Great Britain
- Maureen Connolly ("Little Mo"), tennis star

Cuba in the Sixties

During the 1960s the United States experienced major difficulties with the Caribbean nation of Cuba in two separate but related incidents: the Bay of Pigs invasion and the Cuban Missile Crisis. Read about these events below.

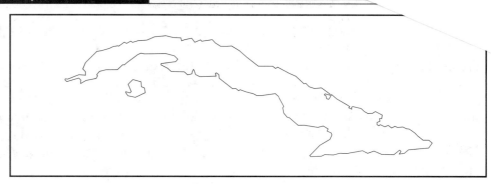

Bay of Pigs, 1961

Fidel Castro seized power in Cuba in 1959 and set up a communist government. This worried the United States because Cuba was so close to their coast. During President Eisenhower's administration, a secret plan was hatched to help oust the dictator. The United States provided training for a group of Cuban exiles but then failed to deliver the necessary support when the plan was actually carried out under President Kennedy. Castro easily defended the Bay of Pigs from the attack. Both the Soviets and the Cubans were angered by this attack while President Kennedy was forced to accept the blame for the failed coup.

Cuban Missile Crisis, 1962

Soviet premier Nikita Khrushchev warned the United States that further attacks in Cuba would be considered an act of war. Then U.S. planes discovered Soviet ships unloading weapons in Cuba and saw missile sites being built. The missiles could easily strike major American cities, and they represented a direct threat to the security of the United States.

On October 22, 1962, President Kennedy demanded that Russia withdraw the missiles or else the United States would attack Cuba. For one week the tension mounted as American warships established a blockade around Cuba to make sure that no new missiles entered the country. American bombers moved into position in Florida, and U.S. troops prepared for a possible invasion of Cuba. On October 28, Khrushchev agreed to remove the missiles if the United States agreed not to invade Cuba. World War III was narrowly averted.

———— Suggested Activities ————

Letter Khrushchev wrote President Kennedy a letter with his offer of removing the missiles from Cuba if Kennedy agreed not to invade the island. Write a letter as Khrushchev, explaining the terms of your offer to President Kennedy.

Research Research the role of the Eisenhower administration in planning the Bay of Pigs invasion. Was Kennedy totally to blame for its subsequent failure?

Decision Making Review background information about the Cuban missile crisis. Brainstorm a number of options available to the U.S. (invade Cuba, bomb Cuba's missile sites, etc.). Discuss the consequences of each. Your class can vote on an option. Discuss Kennedy's choice. **Note:** A great resource for this activity is the book *You Are the President* by Nathan Aaseng (The Oliver Press, Inc., 1994).

Canada's Centennial

July 1, which is Canada Day, was a very special birthday in 1967 because Canada celebrated its centennial, or 100 years in existence.

The nation of Canada was born in 1867. At the request of four colonies in North America—Quebec, Ontario, Nova Scotia, and New Brunswick—the British Parliament passed the British North America Act, now known as the Constitution Act, creating a confederation of these four provinces. Since then, six more provinces and two territories have joined the Dominion of Canada.

What do you know about the government of the great country of Canada? Find out some important facts by unscrambling the letter groups at the beginning of each sentence. Write the word correctly on the line provided. Read the completed facts with a partner.

1. **rcamnho**
   Canada recognizes the British_____as its formal head of state.

2. **semtsy**
   Canada's government is modeled largely on the British parliamentary_____.

3. **rafeedl**
   The 1867 Constitution Act provides for separation of_____and provincial or territorial powers.

4. **esefnde**
   The federal government was given control of areas such as_____, customs, and currency.

5. **tudeoican**
   Provinces retained control of matters of local concern, including_____and civil rights.

6. **toaxitna**
   Some areas, such as immigration and_____, are governed jointly.

7. **turneintw**
   Canada's laws and system of government consist of both written and _____codes.

8. **ntiriBa**
   These unwritten codes include the parliamentary cabinet system which is patterned after the one used in_____.

9. **vegiliatsel**
   This system links two branches of government, the executive and the_____.

10. **cayjruidi**
    A third branch of the government, the_____, is an appointed body.

11. **ibeanct**
    The monarch, the prime minister, and the_____compose the executive branch.

12. **simtrien**
    Actual executive power in Canada is held by the prime_____and his or her cabinet.

Suggested Activity

Comparison Construct a chart to compare the Canadian system of government with that of the United States. Discuss how the two are alike.

Reverence for Life

When he was 21 years old, Albert Schweitzer determined that he would devote his life to serving humanity. Although he was not exactly sure how he would implement his goal, he planned to continue his studies in theology, philosophy, and music until he was 30. He thought that by then he would have his life's work figured out.

Albert Schweitzer was born on January 14, 1875, in Kaysersberg, Alsace, a section of Germany that is now a part of France. His father, Louis Schweitzer, was a clergyman and his mother, Adele Schillinger, was the daughter of a pastor. Louis Schweitzer served as his son's music teacher and taught him how to play the piano. When Albert Schweitzer was 10, he left home to begin his secondary education. An average student, he studied philosophy and theology at Strasbourg University. It was there that he found an answer to his life calling. He opened a missionary magazine to an article titled "The Needs of the Congo Mission," and by the time he had finished reading the story, he knew his search was over.

Albert Schweitzer

In order to practice medicine in Africa, Schweitzer studied tropical medicine. In 1912 he received his M.D. That same year he married Helene Bresslau, a social worker and nurse. For almost a year the young couple made lists of all the necessary supplies they would take with them and raised money for their venture. When they finally arrived in Lambarene in Gabon, they found conditions far worse than they had envisioned. No doctor had been there for many years, and the only building available for use as a hospital was a converted chicken coop. But the clinic was an overwhelming success. Villagers walked miles to see the doctor for all sorts of diseases ranging from malaria to sleeping sickness to leprosy.

When war broke out between Germany and France in 1914, the Schweitzers were held under house arrest. Because Schweitzer had been born in Germany, the French, who now controlled Gabon, considered him an enemy. During this time, he was not allowed to treat patients. Restless, he wrote his first book, *Philosophy of Civilization.* Not for seven more years would he be able to return to his mission in Africa.

Over the years, a large medical complex was built with donations and money that Schweitzer earned by lecturing and writing books. In 1952 he won the Nobel Peace Prize and was able to build a village for leprosy patients with the proceeds. After his wife died, Schweitzer remained in Africa until his death on September 4, 1965. He was 90 years old.

Suggested Activities

Biography Read the whole story about Albert Schweitzer. One recommended resource is *Albert Schweitzer* by Harold E. Robles (The Millbrook Press, 1994).

Goals Discuss current areas of greatest need in the world. In groups, develop a plan for helping others. Share the plan with your class.

The First Heart Transplant

Dr. Christiaan Barnard of South Africa gained international fame when he performed the first heart transplant surgery on December 2, 1967. His patient was Louis Washkansky, a 54-year-old grocer who had life-threatening heart disease. The donor was Denise Duvall, a young woman who suffered fatal injuries in an automobile accident in Cape Town. Because it was the first such operation, little was known about which drugs and how much of them should be used. Mr. Washkansky died of double pneumonia 18 days after his surgery.

One year later, Dr. Barnard performed another heart transplant. This time he placed the heart of a mixed-race stroke victim into a 58-year-old white dentist. Controversy reigned as apartheid was still in effect in South Africa. The patient, however, fared well, and after 74 days in the hospital, was released to go home.

In time, more and more surgeons around the world began to experiment with heart transplants. Dr. Barnard's surgeries were even more successful, and he developed a new type of artificial heart valve. Today, this type of surgery is quite common, but problems of rejection have yet to be overcome.

Suggested Activity

Below you will find a drawing of a human heart. Write the number of each part listed on the correct line. Use reference sources to help you.

1. left atrium
2. inferior vena cava
3. right atrium
4. left pulmonary veins
5. left ventricle
6. superior vena cava
7. aorta
8. bicuspid valve
9. right pulmonary veins
10. semilunar valve
11. tricuspid valve
12. right ventricle
13. pulmonary artery
14. septum

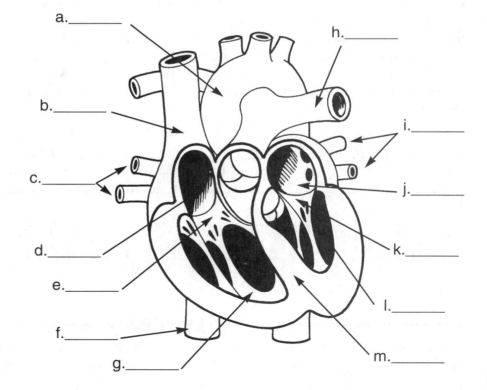

a.____ b.____ c.____ d.____ e.____ f.____ g.____ h.____ i.____ j.____ k.____ l.____ m.____

Answers: Teacher, fold under before copying.
a. 7 b. 6 c. 9 d. 3 e. 11 f. 2 g. 12 h. 13 i. 4 j. 1 k. 8 l. 5 m. 14

Tourists on Antarctica

Tourists have been coming to Antarctica since the late 1950s. As a hotel owner, you envision great possibilities for the region and plan to build a hotel and airstrip there. Among the activities people can enjoy are hiking, skiing, camping, mountain climbing, and driving a dogsled team. They can also see and photograph penguins, elephant seals, and other wildlife.

Environmentalists, however, oppose your plans because they say that tourists pose the biggest threat to the environment of the continent. People inadvertently bother penguin rookeries, use rocks for graffiti, and take penguin eggs or rocks as souvenirs.

In the space at the left, write arguments for allowing visitors to enter Antarctica. In the space at the right, write arguments for discontinuing Antarctic visitors.

For	Against

Two Female Leaders

Golda Meir and Indira Gandhi were leaders of their respective countries during the 1960s. Compare the two by writing the information from the facts list in the correct sections of the Venn diagram below.

Facts List

- attended Oxford University in London
- born in Kiev, Russia
- retired in 1974
- led her country in war with another nation
- elected prime minister of India in 1967
- assassinated in 1984
- was an activist
- grew up in Milwaukee, Wisconsin
- Israel's first minister of labor
- criticized during her administration
- first woman elected to lead a democracy
- at age 12 organized a branch of the "Monkey Brigade"
- acted as her father's official hostess when he was prime minister
- member of the Zionists
- became prime minister after the Six-Day War in 1969
- worked tirelessly for her country
- served as minister of education and broadcasting
- stepped down from prime minister position in favor of Begin

Gandhi	Both	Meir

Answers: (*Fold under before copying*)

Gandhi: attended Oxford . . ., elected prime minister of India . . ., assassinated . . ., first woman elected . . ., at age 12 organized . . ., acted as her father's . . ., served as minister . . . **Both:** led her country in war . . ., was an activist, criticized . . ., worked tirelessly . . .

Meir: born in Kiev . . ., retired in 1974, grew up in Milwaukee. . ., Israel's first . . ., member of the Zionists, became prime minister after . . ., stepped down . . .

Aborigine Rights

In the sixties, Native American civil rights activists in the United States worked to expose the suffering of many Indians. The Native Americans wanted to be involved in the planning and control of the programs that affected them. At the same time on the other side of the globe, another native group, the Aborigines, were receiving similar attention. The Aborigines were an ancient culture in Australia and until the 1960s were not considered Australian citizens. They were not allowed to vote, did not receive full social benefits, and were not even included in their country's census.

Test your knowledge of this ancient civilization by choosing and circling the correct word in each set of parentheses. Use reference resources to help you find correct answers.

1. When white explorers first encountered Aborigines, these Australian natives still lived as they did in the (Stone Age, Bronze Age).

2. Probably the first Aborigines came to Australia 50,000 years ago from (New Zealand, Southeast Asia).

3. Many Aborigines died from the (food, diseases) introduced by the Europeans.

4. Aborigines obtained their own food by hunting animals and (gathering food, herding cattle).

5. Tribespeople wore ornaments and waistbands but little (makeup, clothing).

6. Aborigines had no permanent (housing, farms) because they were always on the move to find food.

7. To protect themselves, they built huts or found protection under (rocks, the ground).

8. Men hunted large animals with spears, traps, and (boomerangs, Frisbees).

9. Women gathered fruits, vegetables, and small animals such as (arachnids, insects) and lizards.

10. Aboriginal art includes stone engravings, paintings done on bark, and (cave paintings, oil paintings).

Suggested Activities

Today Write a description of the Aborigines in Australia today. Explain the Australian government's policy toward the native group.

Compare Compare and contrast the treatment of the Aborigines by the Australian government with the treatment of the Native Americans by the United States government.

Research Find out more about the roles of men and women in the traditional Aborigine tribe. Compare and contrast theim to the roles of men and women today.

- -

Answers: (*Fold under before copying*).

1. Stone Age 2. Southeast Asia 3. diseases 4. gathering food 5. clothing 6. housing 7. rocks 8. boomerangs 9. insects 10. cave paintings

A Famous Sculptor

While pop art, op art, and minimalism are possibly the best known art forms of the sixties, other artists explored other mediums. Henry Moore, a British sculptor, had a strong influence on contemporary figural sculpture.

Moore was born in 1898 in Yorkshire, England. He studied at the Leeds School of Art and at the Royal College of Art in London. His earliest work was influenced by pre-Columbian art form the Americas, Italian Renaissance works of artists like Michelangelo, and the streamlined shapes of French sculptor Brancusi. By the 1930s Moore's work became more abstract, following the influence of Pablo Picasso and other contemporary abstract artists.

The most characteristic subject of Moore's sculptures is the reclining human figure. Other themes include mother and child, family groups, and fallen warriors. His representations range from realistic to abstract. Throughout his career he worked in wood, stone, bronze, and marble.

Moore believed that principles of form and rhythm, which he translated into his sculpture, could be found in natural objects, like pebbles, rocks, bones, trees, and plants. He also believed in "truth to the material," which meant that he respected his medium whether it was wood, metal, or stone. Because of this, his designs seem to emerge effortlessly from the materials and to harmonize with the natural streaks and textures in them.

Many of Moore's works, which are usually very large, can be seen outdoors. Some of his commissioned works are on display at UNESCO Headquarters in Paris, the Lincoln Center for the Performing Arts in New York City, the City Hall of Toronto in Canada, and the East Building of the National Gallery of Art in Washington, D.C.

Suggested Activity

Soap Sculpture Experience sculpting with the project outlined below. You can display completed work in a classroom gallery. To extend this activity, write a brief paragraph about one or more of the other students' sculptures, describing the piece and telling what it means. Discuss the responses.

Materials a bar of soap for each student, small knives, newspaper

Directions

Cover the table or work surface with newspaper. Plan your sculpture. Visualize the figure or face you wish to create and make a sketch. Begin carving, removing a small amount of material at a time to achieve the shape you want. As you work, turn the piece to see how it looks from each side. When you have finished carving, brush off any scrapings.

References

The Annotated Mona Lisa: A Crash Course in Art History from Prehistoric to Post-Modern by Carol Strickland, Ph.D. (Andrews and McMeel, 1992)

People in Art by Anthea Peppin (Merilon Publishing, 1991)

Understanding Modern Art by Monica Bohm-Duchen and Janet Cook (Usborne Publishing, 1988)

The First Woman in Space

In 1961 Yuri Gagarin, a Russian cosmonaut, had become the first man to fly in space, but on June 16, 1963, it was a female's turn for the same feat. On that day, Russia's Valentina V. Tereshkova became the first woman to fly in space. A hero, she gained international attention and was honored with parades and her government's highest honor. Here is her story.

Valentina Tereshkova

Tereshkova was born on March 6, 1937, in a small village near Yaroslavl, a city on the Volga River in the former Soviet Union. From 1939 to 1945, Russia was involved in World War II, and Tereshkova's father was just one of the many casualties. His death left her, her mother, brother, and sister nearly destitute. She was 10 before she began school and was 17 when she became an apprentice at a local tire factory. She continued her studies at night school and soon gained a position at the cotton mill where her mother and sister both worked. In addition, she joined an air sports club and learned how to parachute from planes.

Despite the fact that she had little higher education, Tereshkova wanted more than anything to become a cosmonaut. She wrote to the Soviet space authorities and volunteered for their program. With her parachuting ability and professed love of the cosmonaut program, she was accepted. Training began in 1962, and nine months later she had earned the military rank of junior lieutenant.

Her mission began on June 16, 1963, when she boarded the *Vostok 6* capsule at the Baikonur, Kazakhstan, launchpad. During orbit, Tereshkova communicated with a cosmonaut who was orbiting Earth in another spacecraft. Her time aloft was 70 hours and 50 minutes. From four miles above the Earth she ejected and parachuted safely to the ground. Premier Nikita Khrushchev praised her accomplishment, saying that she had proved that women were not the weaker sex. Not until 1982, however, would another female cosmonaut fly in space.

Valentina Tereshkova remained in the cosmonaut program for several years before retiring to enter politics.

Suggested Activities

Cosmonaut In 1982 Svetlana Savitskaya became the second female Russian cosmonaut in space. Research (see resources below) and find out more about her accomplishments.

Compare How do spacecrafts return to Earth these days? Compare that with the way Savitskaya and her fellow cosmonuats returned during the early days of the space program.

Parachutes In pairs, make parachutes. See Teacher Created Materials #493, *Focus on Scientists,* page 99, for directions. Test the parachutes outdoors.

References

U.S. and Soviet Space Programs: A Comparison by David E. Newton (Franklin Watts, 1988)

Women in Space by Carole S. Brigg (Lerner Publications, 1988)

Berlin's Wall

After World War II ended, Germany was divided into four occupied territories controlled by American, British, French, and Soviet military forces. Allied leaders had agreed to reunite the regions at a future date. Soviet leaders, however, broke their agreements and began building an 866-mile fortified border, dividing Germany into east and west. The west part of Germany became a democratic country while the east portion became a communist state. Allied troops still occupied part of the city of Berlin, however, and it, too, was divided. Its western part became an island of democracy in a communist country.

In 1961 Soviet leader Nikita Khrushchev demanded that the United States pull out of West Berlin, but President Kennedy refused. With neither side willing to budge, it appeared that war was imminent. The communists shocked everyone, however, by building a wall between the sections of the city. Barbed wire was installed on top of the wall, and armed guards were ordered to shoot East Germans who tried to flee to West Berlin.

Not until 1989 was the wall torn down when the communist government of East Germany was overthrown. Nearly 200 people had been killed trying to escape over the wall.

Suggested Activity

Learn about the city of Berlin as it stands today. Use reference materials to help you supply the information requested below.

Population: _____

Size: _____

Ethnic Population: _____

Religion: _____

City Symbol: _____

Two Main Industries: _____

Geography: _____

Highest Point in the City: _____

Answers: (*Fold under before copying*)

Population: 3,100,000; **Size:** 341 square miles (883 sq. km); **Ethnic Population:** German, some Turks, Yugoslavs, Greeks, Italians; **Predominant Religion:** Protestant; **City Symbol:** the bear; **Two Main Industries:** high-tech electronics/chemicals/pharmaceuticals and machine building; **Geography:** lies on a flat plain; **Highest Point in the City:** TV tower at Alexanderplatz

If You Were There

Ask the students to imagine themselves as some of the famous people of the sixties. For example, what might it have been like to be the first woman in space, or how might it have felt to perform the first heart transplant surgery? Discuss these and other hypothetical situations with the class. Have each student choose one of the situations listed below and complete the assignment. Students can share their writings in small groups.

1. Even though you have little higher education, you want to become a cosmonaut. Write a letter to the Soviet space authorities volunteering your services. Tell them about your parachuting abilities and explain how you feel about the cosmonaut program.

2. You are an art critic for the *New York Times* and have been sent to Britain to review Henry Moore's latest work, *Reclining Mother and Child.* Write a news article detailing the flowing lines and hidden beauty of this sculpture.

3. Pretend that you are the young Dr. Albert Schweitzer. For a year you have been planning your clinic in Africa. Although you are not sure what to expect, you are taken aback by what you do find. Write a diary entry about your first day at the clinic site.

4. Sickly as a child, you were never expected to walk. Now you, Wilma Rudolph, are at the 1960 Olympic Games. In 1956 you were part of the bronze medal winning relay team, but today you hope to take home the gold. Write a letter to your mother expressing your hopes for this competition.

5. You are Auguste Piccard, inventor of the bathyscaphe *Trieste,* and you have been invited to speak to a group of sixth graders. Write a speech you will give to the class, explaining how the craft is able to descend to the ocean floor.

6. The city in which you live has just been divided into two sections with a heavily guarded wall. You want to visit your grandparents who live on the other side. Write a plan for a daring balloon escape to visit your grandparents.

7. Because of a life-threatening heart disease, you must undergo a heart transplant. Dr. Christiaan Barnard has been assigned to your case. You know he is a respected surgeon, but you still have some questions. Write a conversation you might have with him before surgery.

8. Recent tests indicate that there might be oil in Antarctica, and your country is sending you there on a fact-finding mission. You are an avid environmentalist and believe that searching for oil may upset the ecological balance. Make a list of your concerns.

9. Advisors are telling you to bomb or invade Cuba, but as president of the United States you are not convinced that either choice is correct. Instead, you set up a blockade to prevent more weapons from entering Cuba. Explain the reasons for your choice to your advisors.

10. When you first see the Aborigines, you can barely believe your eyes. They are living in primitive conditions and have not even invented the wheel yet. In a paper for the geographic society, describe the culture of these ancient people.

Sixties Facts and Figures

The United States in the Sixties

Population:	179,323,175
National Debt:	$289 billion (1961)
Federal Minimum Wage:	raised from $1.25 to $1.40 per hour (1963)
U.S. Postage:	raised from 4 cents to 5 cents (1963)
Popular Books:	*Catch-22* by Joseph Heller; *Portnoy's Complaint* by Philip Roth; *To Kill a Mockingbird* by Harper Lee; *Tropic of Cancer* by Henry Miller; *One Flew Over the Cuckoo's Nest* by Ken Kesey; *Slaughterhouse Five* by Kurt Vonnegut
Popular Movies:	*The Apartment, West Side Story, Lawrence of Arabia, Tom Jones, My Fair Lady, The Sound of Music, A Man for All Seasons, In the Heat of the Night, Oliver, Midnight Cowboy*
Popular Songs:	"Cathy's Clown," "Spanish Harlem," "Only the Lonely," "Moon River," "I Fall to Pieces," "I Left My Heart in San Francisco," "I Want to Hold Your Hand," "Louie Louie," "Hello Dolly," "Satisfaction," "Stop in the Name of Love," "California Dreamin'," "Respect," "Mrs. Robinson," "Aquarius/Let the Sunshine In"
TV Shows:	*The Super Bowls, Star Trek, Rowan and Martin's Laugh-In, Sesame Street* (premieres on PBS in 1969), *The Smothers Brothers, The Dick Van Dyke Show*
Fashions:	miniskirts, paper throwaway clothes, A-line dresses and skirts, loose fitting shifts, Twiggy, pillbox hats, bouffant hairdos
Fads:	face painting, wearing flowers in one's hair, the Twist, the Jerk, lava lamps, waterbeds, Day-Glo and black light, posters, flashing a peace sign
Popular Cars:	Volkswagen bug, '64 Ford Mustang, '63 Corvette Sting Ray, Chevy Bel Air, '64 Plymouth Barracuda, '64 Pontiac GTO
Popular Toys:	skateboards, Frisbees, Twister, Barbie and Ken dolls, G.I. Joe dolls, troll dolls

78

Then and Now Worksheet

With your partner fill in the blanks on this page. Compare your answers with the information on page 78.

U.S. Now _____
(year)

Population _____

National Debt _____

Federal Minimum Wage _____

United States Postage _____

Popular Books _____

Popular Movies _____

Popular Songs _____

Popular TV Shows _____

Fashions _____

Fads _____

Popular Cars _____

Popular Toys _____

Then and Now Follow-Ups

While the information displayed on page 78 is interesting by itself, there are many ways to extend the facts and figures presented. Choose from the following suggestions.

1. **Math** Have the students compare figures from the sixties to the current decade. After they have found the difference between the two decades, students can find the percentage of increase for each category. A prepared worksheet can be found on page 81.

2. **Stars** Some of the movie stars of the sixties are still popular in the American culture, for example, Dustin Hoffman, Clint Eastwood, and Barbra Streisand. Jodie Foster, who later became a movie star, was born in the sixties and had her first acting role on television before the end of the decade. Research and find out more about these performers—in which movies have they appeared, what awards have they received, how did they contribute to the acting world, what have they done beyond acting, etc.

3. **Cars** By the end of the late twenties almost every household had an automobile. By the late sixties there was nearly one car for every two people. Instruct the students to find out current figures about cars and the United States population. What factors have contributed to the increase?

4. **Rock On** Many of the sixties rock bands continued to enjoy success into the nineties, for example, the Grateful Dead, the Rolling Stones, the Beach Boys, and Pink Floyd. Listen to some of the groups' early albums from the sixties and compare them with their current music. Describe how the lyrics and music have changed.

5. **Clothes** Fashions changed considerably during the sixties with the advent of the miniskirt, throwaway clothes, and plastic clothing. Instruct the students to find pictures of some other sixties fashion crazes. Divide the class into groups and have them draw collages of fashions.

6. **Fads** Face painting and wearing flowers in one's hair were two fads initiated by the counterculture of the 1960s. With the class discuss what these fads represented and the groups that initiated them.

7. **TV** Examine the list of sixties television shows. Are the students familiar with any of them? What do they think of these shows compared to those that appear on television today?

8. **Wages** In 1963 the federal minimum wage was raised to $1.40 per hour. Ask students what they can buy today for $1.40. Pair the students and have them make a list of things that cost $1.40 at the grocery store or a department store.

9. **The Twist** The Twist was a popular dance in the early sixties. Chubby Checker's hit "Let's Twist Again" launched a worldwide dance fad. It also started a new form of dance in which couples faced one another but did not touch. Teach the students how to do the Twist (invite a ballroom dance teacher to show the class how). Learn about some other dance crazes of the sixties: the Swim, the Watusi, and the Jerk.

Then and Now Math

Compare these facts and figures of the sixties with current ones. First, in each category find past and current figures to write in the blanks. Next, find the difference between the figures. Finally, figure the percentage of increase in each sample.

1. United States Population in

   1960_____

   United States Population now_____

   Difference_____

   % Increase_____

4. United States Postage in

   1963 _____

   United States Postage now _____

   Difference _____

   % Increase_____

2. National Debt in 1961_____

   National Debt now_____

   Difference_____

   % Increase_____

5. Price of One Loaf of Bread in

   196___   _____

   Price of One Loaf of Bread now _____

   Difference _____

   % Increase_____

3. Federal Minimum Wage in

   1963_____

   Federal Minimum Wage now_____

   Difference_____

   % Increase_____

6. Price of a Gallon of Milk in

   196___   _____

   Price of a Gallon of Milk now_____

   Difference _____

   % Increase_____

Famous Firsts

Every era has its famous firsts, and the sixties is no exception. On this page you will find a number of firsts along with a brief discussion of each. After each one, write about the improvements or advances that have been made in that area today.

Heart Transplant In 1967 the first successful heart transplant operation was performed by Dr. Christiaan Barnard of South Africa. The heart of a 25-year old accident victim was placed in the body of heart-disease patient Louis Washansky, but the procedure was not entirely successful. Washkansky died of pneumonia less than three weeks later. _____

_____

_____

Giant Bridge The Verrazano-Narrows bridge opened in New York in November of 1964. It stretched 4,260 feet across the entrance to New York City harbor, from Staten Island to Brooklyn. At the time, it was the world's longest suspension bridge. _____

_____

The Minidress Flappers of the Roaring Twenties wore short hemlines which shocked their elders, but they could not compare to the minidresses sported by women in the sixties. Midthigh length skirts became a symbol of the rebellious decade's younger generation. _____

_____

_____

Ocean Depths In 1960 the submersible *Trieste* descended nearly seven miles to the bottom of the Mariana Trench, the deepest part of the Pacific Ocean. The journey down to the bottom of the ocean floor took five hours. _____

_____

Endangered Species The Department of the Interior issued its first endangered species list on March 1, 1967. Included in the list were 78 birds and animals that were threatened with extinction.

_____

_____

Trekkies On September 8, 1966, the science fiction series *Star Trek* premiered on the NBC television network. Although it only ran for three seasons, it has continued to be popular in reruns and has amassed a huge following of devoted fans (once called "Trekkies" and now called "Trekers"). By the mid-nineties, the show had spawned several feature films and three other television series.

_____

_____

_____

In the Middle

All of the sixties figures described in the sentences below have three names. Notice that their middle names are missing.

Find the correct middle names from the box and write them in the proper spaces.

Baines	Francis	David	Scott	Edgar	Jean
Harvey	Earl	Milhous	Luther	Bouvier	Fitzgerald

1. Richard _____ Nixon was the first president to resign from office.

2. On April 4, 1968, James _____ Ray assassinated Dr. King.

3. As head of the FBI, J. _____ Hoover sometimes planted false articles in newspapers.

4. John _____ Kennedy was the first president to be born in the twentieth century.

5. During Dwight _____ Eisenhower's presidency, Cuban exiles were secretly trained by the CIA.

6. Billie _____ King won three consecutive Wimbledons during the sixties.

7. Accused assassin Lee _____ Oswald was killed by Jack Ruby before he could be tried.

8. Lyndon _____ Johnson was sworn in as chief executive aboard *Air Force One*.

9. Martin _____ King, Jr., is famous for his "I have a dream..." speech.

10. First Lady Jacqueline _____ Kennedy led 47 million viewers on a televised tour of the White House.

11. Coretta _____ King demonstrated for peace alongside her husband Martin.

12. Robert _____ Kennedy served in his older brother's cabinet as United States attorney general.

Paper Battleship

The game Battleship first appeared in 1967. Although it had been in production continually since then, the game enjoyed a resurgence in popularity in the 1990s. Students can play a paper and pencil version of Battleship with the game below.

Preparation

1. Two can play this game; each partner will need a copy of the grid section below.

2. Mark dots on the grid at intersecting points to represent each ship. For example, the carrier has four bombing points, so draw dots at four intersecting points, all in a row, anywhere on the grid. Draw the carrier outline around the dots as shown in the diagrams. The points can be lined up horizontally, vertically, or diagonally.

3. Place the remaining ships on the grid in the same manner.

To Play Have the players conceal their grids from one another (students can place a file folder upright between them). One partner begins by calling out a coordinate (B-5, for example) for a "bomb." If the "bomb" misses his partner's ships, the partner calls out "missed." But if the "bomb" lands on a coordinate of one of the ships, the partner says "hit." The caller then marks an X or other symbol on his own grid to keep track of his hits. Players take turns calling out coordinates. The winner is the fist person to "sink" all of his enemy's ships.

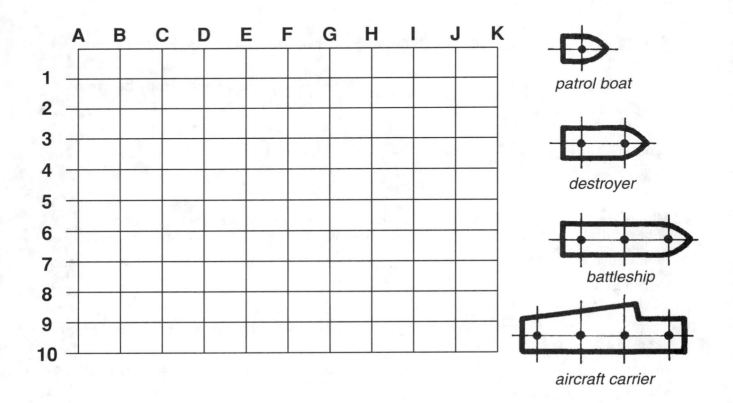

patrol boat

destroyer

battleship

aircraft carrier

What Year Was That?

Check how well you remember the events of the sixties with this quiz. After each number read the three clues given. Decide in what year all three events occurred. Circle the letters of your answers.

1. Betty Friedan founds NOW. Congress creates a new executive department, Housing and Urban Development. LSD is introduced into United States culture.
           a. 1965   b. 1966   c. 1967

2. The March on Washington is held. President Kennedy is assassinated. A vaccine for measles is discovered.
           a. 1962   b. 1963   c. 1964

3. The Berlin Wall is built. The Bay of Pigs invasion fails. The Peace Corps is founded.
           a. 1960   b. 1961   c. 1962

4. Richard Nixon is inaugurated as president. The Woodstock Music and Art Fair draws a crowd of 400,000. Astronauts walk on the moon.
           a. 1967   b. 1968   c. 1969

5. Martin Luther King, Jr. is assassinated. North Vietnam launches Tet offensive. North Korea seizes USS *Pueblo*.
           a. 1966   b. 1967   c. 1968

6. Chavez forms the United Farm Workers. The 50-star United States flag becomes official. The first sit-in is held.
           a. 1960   b. 1961   c. 1962

7. The counterculture celebrates the "summer of love." The Twenty-fifth Amendment is ratified. Three astronauts are killed at Cape Kennedy.
           a. 1965   b. 1966   c. 1967

8. NASA launches *Telstar*. The Twenty-fourth Amendment is approved. The Cuban Missile Crisis occurs.
           a. 1961   b. 1962   c. 1963

9. Race riots erupt in Watts. The Voting Rights Act is passed. President Johnson launches Great Society programs.
           a. 1965   b. 1966   c. 1967

10. Johnson declares "War on Poverty." The Beatles make their first United States appearance. The Civil Rights Act is passed.
            a. 1963   b. 1964   c. 1965

11. Miranda Rights are instituted. The first African American cabinet member is appointed. A teach-in is held to protest the Vietnam War.
            a. 1964   b. 1965   c. 1966

12. Monterey Pop Festival is initiated. The first successful human heart transplant takes place. Pulsars are discovered.
            a. 1967   b. 1968   c. 1969

On into the Seventies

- The political and social turmoil of the late 1960s continued into the seventies.
- American and South Vietnamese forces entered Cambodia and Laos in 1970 in an attempt to cut North Vietnamese supply lines.
- At Kent State University, students protesting the bombing of Cambodia set fire to an ROTC (Reserve Officers Training Corps) building. Called to stop the riot, National Guardsmen opened fire, wounding eight and killing four.
- In a new offensive, North Vietnamese soldiers crossed into Quang Tri province but were stopped by the South Vietnamese. Bombing of North Vietnam by U.S. planes, halted in 1968, resumed in 1972 with railroads and supply lines as principal targets. The harbor at Haiphong was also mined.
- Although peace talks between Henry Kissinger of the United States and Le Duc Tho of North Vietnam began in Paris in 1970, fighting continued until the cease-fire agreement was reached in 1973.
- U.S. troops withdrew from Vietnam in 1973 and from Laos in 1974. In 1975 Saigon fell to the North Vietnamese. The same year, the communist Khmer Rouge came to power in Cambodia, and the Pathet Lao took over the government of Laos.
- In 1971 the publication of *The Pentagon Papers*, a history of the Vietnam War, added to antiwar sentiments by revealing that the government had not been completely honest.
- A court martial convicted Lt. William Calley and sentenced him to life in prison for his role in the "My Lai Massacre" of 1968 in which 22 unarmed Vietnamese civilians were killed.
- Early in 1973 the trial of seven men accused of the 1972 break-in and wiretapping of the National Democratic Committee offices in the Watergate building began. Eventually this scandal spread to include members of the president's cabinet and staff and brought the threat of impeachment to President Richard Nixon.
- Spiro Agnew, accused of bribery, conspiracy, and tax evasion, resigned the vice presidency in October 1973. At his trial he pleaded *nolo contendre* and was fined and given probation.
- President Nixon named Gerald Ford, U.S. Representative from Michigan to succeed Agnew. This was the first time the Twenty-fifth Amendment, passed in 1967, was applied.
- In 1974 Richard M. Nixon resigned the presidency. New president Gerald Ford nominated Nelson Rockefeller to fill the office of vice president.
- By 1976 people were quick to embrace Jimmy Carter with his homespun message of peace and hope as their new president.
- Revelations of misdeeds in government left the activists of the sixties frustrated and disillusioned. They turned their energies inward, embracing fitness, health foods, and transcendental meditation. Some have called the seventies the "Me Decade."
- Throughout the seventies, the women's movement grew stronger as leaders, including Gloria Steinem and Kate Millet, led the revolution. New opportunities were opened to women, and many left the safety of the home to find fulfillment in the workplace.
- In the 1973 landmark Supreme Court decision Roe v. Wade, women were granted abortion rights. A controversial topic, the debate has continued well into the nineties.
- The Arab oil embargo against the Western world had a severe effect on the economy. One effect was a new concern for the environment. Natural foods and fabrics gained popularity, and preventing air pollution and preserving the environment were important growing trends.

For Discussion

How has the women's movement impacted women's lives today?

Does an underlying distrust of the government linger in America today from the Watergate affair?

Is concern for the environment currently a major issue?

Literature Connections

One surefire way to interest students in a specific topic is through the use of children's literature. Read through the annotated bibliographies to help you decide which pieces of literature you might like to use with your class. Helpful suggestions for extending the pages follow each description.

The Story of Ruby Bridges by Robert Coles (Scholastic, Inc., 1995)
The Supreme Court decision in the *Brown v. Board of Education* case in 1954 provided for integration of all public schools. Many Southern communities refused to comply, and some even closed their schools rather than comply to the new ruling. This struggle continued on into the sixties when civil rights became a key issue.

The Story of Ruby Bridges relates the experiences of six-year-old African American Ruby Bridges. She faces angry protestors daily and is escorted to and from school by federal marshals. With atypical courage and grace for such a young child, Ruby sets an example for all Americans and becomes an unforgettable part of American history.

Extensions

Introduction Use this read aloud book as an introduction to the topic of civil rights and integration in the sixties. Discuss with students the impact of integration on our nation's schools.

Painting Ruby's experience inspired painter Norman Rockwell's 1964 *The Problem We All Live With*. Display a copy of the picture. Have students write a story telling how Ruby might have felt at the time captured in the picture.

Future Ask the students to speculate about what happened to Ruby Bridges. For an update about Ruby—now Ruby Bridges Brown—read the article "Keeper of the Flame" in the December 4, 1995, issue of *People* magazine.

Research Have the students research how the *Brown v. Board of Education* decision affected their own school district.

Charlie Pippin by Candy Dawson Boyd (Macmillan Publishing Company, 1987)
Chartreuse "Charlie" Pippin cannot understand why her father is so hard on her. He never seems to yell at her older sister Sienna. True, she has gotten into trouble at school for setting up a business, but that does not explain his terrible outbursts. Charlie's mom offers her a clue to understanding her dad's behavior. He had fought in Vietnam years ago, and ever since then he has been a changed man. A project at school helps Charlie uncover her father's secret. Her role on the war and peace committee is to study the Vietnam War. What she finds out helps the whole family to heal.

Extensions

Origami Charlie made a variety of origami animals. Teach the students how to make an origami figure. For directions see Teacher Created Materials #233, *Thematic Unit—Peace*.

Sisters Sienna was Charlie's 15-year old sister. Ask the students to describe the girls' relationship, interests, and personalities. Which sister do they like better? Why?

Math At her school Charlie sold 2 pencils for 14 cents. How much are pencils now? What can you buy for 14 cents?

Dreams In a conversation with Charlie, Mama Bliss tells her that "war kills dreams." Reread their conversation on page 38 of *Charlie Pippin*. With the whole group discuss what the quote means.

Literature Connections *(cont.)*

Charlie Pippin *(cont.)*

Fact or Opinion On page 49 of the book, Charlie's father argues with his brother Ben about the Vietnam War and claims that black men died ". . . far more than was just or right." With the students discuss whether this statement is fact or opinion (recommended resource: *Vietnam War Soldiers* by Neil Super, Twenty-First Century Books, 1993). Pair the students and have them find five factual statements and five opinions from the text of *Charlie Pippin*.

Raising Money Mrs. Hayamoto's class decided to raise money for the African relief fund with a Winter Holiday Bazaar. Charlie suggested that the students be allowed to keep a portion of the profits. Conduct a class debate to discuss whether or not students should be able to profit from the fundraiser.

Problems and Solutions With the class identify one problem faced by Charlie or Sienna. Discuss the solution chosen and the consequences which followed. Ask students for their ideas about a better solution to the problem. Divide the class into pairs and direct them to identify a different problem. Have them record their responses on the Problem/Solution Chart below.

Problem/Solution Chart

1. List the character's name. _____

2. Describe a problem the character faces. _____
   _____
   _____
   _____

3. Explain how the character solves the problem. _____
   _____
   _____
   _____

4. Tell the consequences of this solution. _____
   _____
   _____
   _____

5. Identify a better solution to this problem. _____
   _____
   _____
   _____

December Stillness by Mary Downing Hahn (Clarion Books, 1988)
When her social studies teacher assigns the class to write a paper on a contemporary issue, Kelly chooses the homeless for her topic. She focuses on Mr. Weems, the bearded Vietnam vet who carries all of his possessions in two plastic garbage bags and spends most of his time in the town's library. Mr. Weems, however, does not want to be interviewed and rebuffs Kelly's offers of help. When some patrons want Weems barred from the library, Kelly defends him. In her zeal to correct a seeming injustice, Kelly inadvertently contributes to a tragic incident. This is a great book for examining the aftermath of the Vietnam War.

Extensions

Music To set the mood for this book, listen to some music of the sixties by Bob Dylan, The Moody Blues, the Beatles, Cat Stevens, and Joni Mitchell (see page 138 of *December Stillness* for more names).

Interview When Kelly first sees the vet at the library, she decides to interview him for her report. Pair the students and have them role-play—one is the interviewer and the other is the homeless person. Let the students change roles.

Poem Page 36 of the book refers to Shel Silverstein's poem "What's in the Sack?" from *Where the Sidewalk Ends*. Before reading the poem aloud to students, have them speculate about what they think is in Mr. Weems' sacks.

Relationships Assign students to describe how the relationship between Julie and Kelly changes over the course of the story. Students can create a flow chart, write a composition, or draw a story map to identify these changes.

Post-war Kelly discovers that Mr. Weems is suffering from something called posttraumatic stress disorder. Tell the students to research what it is, describe its symptoms, and tell what can be done about it. Discuss their findings in whole group.

Memorial Kelly pays a final tribute to Mr. Weems by leaving a picture she has drawn and a poem she has written next to the Vietnam War Memorial. Instruct the students to draw their own pictures of Mr. Weems and write a poem in his memory.

Comparisons Compare the main characters, setting, plot, action, and resolution of *December Stillness* with *Charlie Pippin*.

Other literature selections you may want to try include the following:

. . . If You Lived at the Time of Martin Luther King by Ellen Levine (Scholastic, Inc., 1994). Its question and answer format will keep students interested.

A Wall of Names by Judy Donnelly (Random House, 1991). This tells the story of the funding and building of the Vietnam Memorial.

Park's Quest by Katherine Paterson (Dutton, New York, 1988). Park determines to find out about his father who was killed in Vietnam.

Creative Writing Prompts

The people, places, and events of the sixties lend themselves to some interesting creative writing prompts. Use them for journal writing or as daily writing exercises. Some sample ideas are presented below.

1. During the sixties Charles Schulz wrote a book titled *Happiness Is a Warm Puppy*. Create your own *Happiness Is . . .* book. Write "Happiness" Is at the top of 10 separate sheets of paper. Write a different definition for happiness on each page; illustrate.

2. Jacqueline Kennedy's style inspired the Jackie look. Describe this look to someone who has never seen a pillbox hat or bouffant hairdo.

3. During his inaugural ceremonies President Kennedy invited poet Robert Frost to recite a poem. Find and read a poem written by Robert Frost. Write your own inaugural poem.

4. Martin Luther King, Jr., is famous for his "I have a dream . . ." speech. Find and read a transcript of the speech. Write a paragraph that begins with "I have a dream . . ."

5. Pretend you have been chosen to be the first to walk on the moon's surface during the *Apollo 11* mission. Write a little speech you will deliver to your fellow Americans as you step into history.

6. The Beatles are making their first American appearance on TV. You and your friends are in the audience. Girls scream, and the noise is deafening as the group sings. Write a list of 19 things you might hear others in the audience saying about the group.

7. In his inaugural speech, John F. Kennedy said, "Ask not what your country can do for you, ask what you can do for your country." If the current president delivered that same message today, what would you do for your country? Write a letter to the president explaining your actions.

8. The 1968 hit musical *Hair* told of a young American on his way to enlist for service in Vietnam. He encounters a group of hippies in New York's Central Park who try to discourage him. Write a one-act play about this man and what the hippies say to him.

9. Three common catch-phrases during the sixties were "Make love, not war," "Whatever turns you on," and "Turn on, tune in, drop out." Draw a poster illustrating one of these phrases, and write some ad copy to accompany your drawing.

10. The space race was on in full force during the sixties. Although the Soviets were the first to travel successfully in space, it was the Americans who landed first on the moon. Write a story explaining the importance of winning this race.

11. In 1969 Thor Heyerdahl sailed from North Africa to the Caribbean. Read about his journey and then write a diary entry telling about an adventure he might have had.

12. Ralph Nader exposed serious safety problems in General Motors cars in his 1966 book *Unsafe at Any Speed*. Write a chapter for an updated version of his book.

90

Square Book Reports

Assign book reports after students have read a suggested 1960s literature selection (see pages 87–89 for some samples). For a change of pace, substitute the activities on the chart below for the traditional written book report. In order to finish a square book report, students must complete one project from each section of the square. If you wish, students may be divided into groups of four. Each member of the group can complete an activity from one section.

Written

1. Rewrite the story ending.
2. Make a list of characteristics of one of the main characters. Choose one and write about an event which illustrates that characteristic.
3. Write a poem which describes one of the characters.

Oral

1. Deliver a persuasive speech to your classmates to convince them to read this book.
2. Give an oral report about one of the characters, explaining his or her role in the story.
3. Read aloud a section from the story that has to do with a problem faced by the main character. In your own words explain how the problem is resolved.

Illustration

1. Draw a story map to show the characters, plot, action, and resolution.
2. Create a new book jacket appropriate for the book.
3. Illustrate a time line of important events in the story.

Etc.

1. Make up "Who Am I?" questions about five different characters. Choose a partner who has read the book and see if he or she can guess the names of the characters.
2. Make a trading card for each of three characters in the book. Include a brief biography and illustration of each.
3. Invent a board game incorporating the characters and events of the story. Let a small group of classmates try out the game.

A Sixties Who's Who

Each of the figures below contributed something important to society in the 1960s. Read through their names and accomplishments. Choose one that you would like to research further and write a one-page report, or read a biography about your choice and complete a square book report (see page 91).

Andy Warhol, best known for his pop art painting of 100 soup cans

Jackie Kennedy, first lady who guided the historical restoration of the White House

Wilma Rudolph, winner of three Olympic gold medals

Thurgood Marshall, the first African American appointed to the United States Supreme Court

Cesar Chavez, the Mexican American who united the migrant farm workers

Rachel Carson, the environmentalist who warned about the dangers of DDT

Richard Wright, a great black novelist of his time

John F. Kennedy, the fourth president to be killed in office

The Beatles, the English rock group whose musical influences can still be felt today

Sidney Poitier, the first African American to win an Oscar for best actor

Jim Henson, creator of the Muppets

Roberto Clemente, humanitarian and great baseball player

Joan Baez, folk singer noted for her protest songs

Shirley Chisholm, the first black Congresswoman

Richard Nixon, the first American president to resign from office

Betty Friedan, founder of NOW and the women's liberation movement

Martin Luther King, Jr., slain civil rights leader

Neil Armstrong, the first person to walk on the moon

Nikki Giovanni, African American poet who promotes racial pride

Lyndon Johnson, former president who initiated a Great Society

Marilyn Monroe, blonde actress who became a pop icon after her death

Malcolm X, slain Black Muslim leader

Robert Frost, winner of four Pulitzer Prizes for poetry and President Kennedy's favorite poet

Dr. Christiaan Barnard, pioneer heart surgeon

Jimi Hendrix, pioneering African American guitarist

Billie Jean King, three-time Wimbledon champion

Charles Schulz, creator of a gang of favorite cartoon characters

Van Cliburn, first American concert pianist to win the Pulitzer Prize who played at a Johnson inaugural party

W.E.B. DuBois, black writer and activist who helped found the NAACP

Buzzwords

Baby Boomer This term refers to people born during the baby boom of the late 1940s, who became teenagers in the 1960s.

Boutiques This French word for "shop" was used to describe the new clothing stores which catered to the youth market.

Commune This describes a group of people who live together and share everything from chores to decisions to childcare.

Communism This is an economic idea in which the government takes charge of and owns its nations' businesses. It is the government that controls work and distributes the nation's goods and services.

Counterculture Groups that rejected the Establishment (all symbols of authority, especially the government and parents) were known by this term.

Doves This is the name given to those who did not want to see more United States involvement in Vietnam.

Drop Out Used as a verb, it means to refuse to take part in society, e.g., refusing to finish school or to get a job.

Feminist This term refers to a person who believes that women should have the same rights and opportunities as men.

Hallucinogens This is the name of a category of drugs which produce hallucinations or sights and sounds that are not really present, e.g., LSD.

Hawks This is the name given to people who wanted to send bombs and fighting troops to Vietnam.

Hippies This was the name given to members of the counterculture. They rejected conventional standards and customs of society, supported liberal ideas, marched in protest, and demanded power at their schools and colleges.

LSD This hallucinogenic drug, popular in the counterculture movement, was banned in 1966.

MIA These initials stand for "missing in action." They were used to describe those who could not be accounted for in Vietnam.

Miniskirts These short, short skirts became a new fashion craze in the sixties.

NOW These initials stand for the National Organization of Women. Under Betty Friedan's guidance its members worked toward women's liberation and equality for women.

Peace Corps This federal program was initiated by President Kennedy in 1961. Volunteers worked two-year stints in Third World countries.

POW This abbreviation stands for "prisoners of war".

Protest Singers These were folk singers who wrote and sang songs about social problems and injustices.

Psychedelic This word describes anything related to hallucinations or altered states of awareness induced by the use of drugs.

Sit-in In this nonviolent demonstration, participants sat at lunch counters to protest the fact that blacks were not allowed to sit at store lunch counters with whites.

Summer of Love Hippies gathered in San Francisco, California, in the summer of 1967.

Unisex Clothing This refers to clothing, such as jeans and T-shirts, designed to be worn by either sex.

Software in the Classroom

More and more software is finding its way into the classroom. Many of the multimedia packages allow students to access photos, speeches, film clips, maps, and newspapers of various eras in history. Although a program may not be written specifically for the topic you are studying, existing software may be adapted for your purposes. To get maximum use from these programs and to learn how to keep up with technology, try some of the suggestions below.

Software

American Heritage: The History of the United States for Young People. Byron Preiss Multimedia

American History CD. Multi-Educator

Blockbuster Video Guide to Movies & Videos. Creative Multimedia

The Chronicle. Sunburst Communications

Compton's Encyclopedia of American History. McGraw Hill

Compton's Interactive Encyclopedia from Compton's New Media, Inc.

The Cruncher. Microsoft Works

Encarta (various editions). Microsoft Home

Ideas That Changed the World. Ice Publishing

The JFK Assassination. Medio

Our Times: Multimedia Encyclopedia of the 20th Century (Vicarious Point of View Series 2.0). Scholastic

Presidents: A Picture History of Our Nation. National Geographic

Time Almanac. Compact Publishing, available through Broderbund, 800-922-9204

TimeLiner from Tom Snyder Productions, 800-342-0236

Time Traveler CD! Orange Cherry

Vital Links. Educational Resources (includes videodisc and audio cassette)

Where in America's Past is Carmen Sandiego? Broderbund

Using the Programs

After the initial excitement of using a new computer program wears off, you can still motivate students by letting them use the programs in different ways.

1. Print out a copy of a time line for the sixties for each group of students. Assign each group a different topic, e.g., entertainment, politics, etc. Direct the groups to research their topics and add text and pictures to their time lines.

2. Let each pair of students choose a specific photo from the 1960s. Have them research the event and write a news story to go with the picture.

3. Not enough computers? Hook your computer up to a TV screen for large-group activities or pair the students and let them take turns typing. Keep a kitchen timer handy. For more ideas see *Managing Technology in the Classroom* from Teacher Created Materials or the booklet *101+ Ways to Use a Computer in the Classroom* (Oxbow Creek Technology Committee, Oxbow Creek School, 6050 109th Ave. N., Champlin, MN 55316).

Internet

If you have access to the Internet, let the students search for related information. First ask the students to brainstorm a list of keywords or topics. Use a Web browser like Alta Vista or Web Crawler to search for sites. Facts, pictures, and sound clips are only a click away. As an alternative, you may wish to preview sites and provide students with a list of URLs for access.

Note: If the students will be searching, you may wish to install a filtering program, like *SurfWatch* from Spyglass, to limit access to objectionable material. Check with your Internet service provider.

Keeping Current

To keep current with the ever-expanding list of available software programs, you may have to turn to a number of sources, including the ones below.

Magazines: *Instructor* and *Learning* (technology review columns and feature articles) *Children's Software Revue* 520 North Adams Street Ypsilanti, Michigan 48197-2482. (Write for a free sample.) *PC Family* and *PC Kids* (available at newsstands).

Books: *Great Teaching and the One-Computer Classroom* (Tom Snyder Productions, Inc., 800-342-0236).

Internet for Kids! by Ted Pederson and Francis Moss (Price Stern Sloan, Inc., 1995). *That's Edutainment!* by Eric Brown (Osborne/McGraw, 1994).

Bibliography

Note: All books marked by an asterisk (*) are Newbery winners from the sixties.

Aaseng, Nathan. *You Are the President.* (Oliver Press, Inc., 1994)

*Alexander, Lloyd. *The High King.* (Dell, 1990)

Ashabranner, Brent K. *Always to Remember: The Story of the Vietnam Memorial.* (Dodd, Mead, 1988)

Bray, Rosemary L. *Martin Luther King.* (Greenwillow Books, 1995)

*de Trevino, Elizabeth Barton. *I, Juan de Pareja.* (Farrar, Strauss, & Giroux, 1984)

Denam, Cherry. *The History Puzzle: An Interactive Visual Timeline.* (Turner Publishing, Inc., 1995)

Felder, Deborah G. *The Kids' World Almanac of History.* (Pharos Books. A Scripps Howard Company, 1991)

Grey, Edward. *The Sixties.* (Steck-Vaughn, 1990)

Hakim, Joy. *All the People.* (Oxford University Press, 1995)

Harrison, Barbard and Daniel Terris. *The Twilight Struggle: The Life of John Fitzgerald Kennedy.* (Lothrop, Lee & Shepard Books, 1992)

Healy, Tim. *Picture History of the 20th Century. The 1960s.* (Franklin Watts, 1988)

Hopkinson, Christina. *The Usborne History of the Twentieth Century.* (Usborne Publishing, Ltd., 1993)

*Hunt, Irene. *Up a Road Slowly.* (Berkley Publishers, 1990)

*Konigsburg, E.L. *From the Mixed-Up Files of Mrs. Basil E. Frankweiler.* (Dell, 1997)

Kranz, Rachel. *The Biographical Dictionary of Black Americans.* (Facts on File, 1992)

*Krumgold, Joseph. *Onion John.* (Harper Trophy, 1984)

Lawson, D. *An Album of the Vietnam War.* (Watts, 1986)

*L'Engle, Madeline. *A Wrinkle in Time.* (Dell, 1997)

Levine, Ellen. *. . . If You Lived at the Time of Martin Luther King.* (Scholastic, 1994)

*Neville, Emily. *It's Like This, Cat.* (Harpercollins, 1992)

*O'Dell, Scott. *The Island of the Blue Dolphins.* (Dell, 1997)

The Oxford Children's Book of Famous People (Oxford University Press, 1994)

Platt, Richard. *The Smithsonian Visual Timeline of Inventions.* (Dorling Kindersley, 1994)

Pradt, Mary A. *You Must Remember This.* (Warner Books, 1995)

Provenson, Alice. *My Fellow Americans.* (Harcourt, Brace and Company, 1995)

Rubel, David. *Encyclopedia of the Presidents and Their Times.* (Scholastic, Inc., 1994)

_____. *The United States in the 20th Century.* (Scholastic, Inc., 1995)

Skarmeas, Nancy. *First Ladies of the White House.* (Ideals Publications Incorporated, 1995)

Smith, Carter, ed. *Presidents in a Time of Change.* (The Millbrook Press, 1993)

*Speare, Elizabeth. *Bronze Bow.* (Houghton Mifflin, 1997)

*Wojciechonska, Maria. *Shadow of a Bull.* (Aladdin Paperbacks, 1992)

Wright, David K. *War in Vietnam.* Books I–IV. (Children's Press, 1989)

Teacher Created Materials

#064 *Share the Olympic Dream*

#069 *Elections*

#233 *Thematic Unit—Peace*

#472 *Learning Through Literature—U.S. History*

#473 *Learning Through Literature—Social Studies*

#517 *Managing Technology in the Classroom*

#605 *Interdisciplinary Unit—Heroes*

Answer Key

Page 21
1. d
2. f
3. a
4. h
5. e
6. b
7. g
8. c

Page 22
Mamie: proud to be a housewife; served the longest as First Lady; known for her trademark pink; nurtured her husband during his frequent illnesses

Jackie: bouffant hairdos and pillbox hats; historically correct renovation of the White House; one of the youngest first ladies ever; led the nation with grace and courage after her husband's death

Lady Bird: beautifying America's landscape; daughters were Lynda and Luci; the Highway Beautification Act; traveled to support the Great Society programs

Pat: supported the cause of volunteerism; the first president's wife to travel to Africa; daughters were Julie and Tricia; greeted tourists visiting the White House

Page 26
1. 1
2. 70,304,422; 538
3. 11,341,436
4. 102,460,163
5. 72,960,802
6. 114,673

Page 28
1. South Vietnam
2. North Vietnam
3. Communist China
4. Ho Chi Minh Trail
5. Laos
6. Cambodia
7. Hue
8. Khesanh

Page 30
My bed is concrete. I have a bucket for a toilet. I am being tortured both mentally and physically.

Page 31
1. 1969
2. 1972
3. 473,000
4. 1968
5. 1967, 1968, 1969
6. 1,167
7. 47,988
8. 2,583,000
9. 1.6%
10. 3.3%

Page 49
Answers may vary. Check for appropriate responses.

Page 50

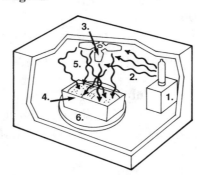

Page 61
Across:
2. bouffant
6. paper
7. pillbox
9. bell-bottoms
12. dutch boy
14. sandals
15. plastic
16. jeans
17. caftans

Down:
1. poppit beads
3. afro
4. bathing suit
5. boots
8. hiphuggers
10. miniskirt
11. tie-dyes
13. tights

Page 65
1. Dawn Fraser
2. Peggy Fleming
3. Madeline Manning
4. Wilma Rudolph
5. Lydia Skoblikova
6. Vera Caslavska
7. Wyomia Tyus
8. Larissa Latynina
9. Carol Heiss
10. Otrun Enderlein
11. Willye White
12. Enriquetta Bassilio

Page 68
1. monarch
2. system
3. federal
4. defense
5. education
6. taxation
7. unwritten
8. Britain
9. legislative
10. judiciary
11. cabinet
12. minister

Page 83
1. Milhous
2. Earl
3. Edgar
4. Fitzgerald
5. David
6. Jean
7. Harvey
8. Baines
9. Luther
10. Bouvier
11. Scott
12. Francis

Page 85
1. 1966
2. 1963
3. 1961
4. 1969
5. 1968
6. 1960
7. 1967
8. 1962
9. 1965
10. 1964
11. 1966
12. 1967